An Honest Living

AN HONEST LIVING

A Memoir of Peculiar Itineraries

Steven Salaita

Fordham University Press   New York   2024

Fordham University Press has no responsibility for the persistence or accuracy of URLs for external or third-party Internet websites referred to in this publication and does not guarantee that any content on such websites is, or will remain, accurate or appropriate.

Fordham University Press also publishes its books in a variety of electronic formats. Some content that appears in print may not be available in electronic books.

Visit us online at www.fordhampress.com.

Library of Congress Cataloging-in-Publication Data available online at https://catalog.loc.gov.

Printed in the United States of America

26 25 24   5 4 3 2 1

First edition

With tremendous gratitude to Tahia Abdel-Nasser, Cynthia Franklin, David Lloyd, Adam Miyashiro, Richard Morrison, Danya Salaita, Matthew Shenoda, and Team 27 of FCPS Transportation Services. All defects and infelicities are my responsibility alone.

For Diana, fighter, butterfly.

Contents

Contents

An Honest Living

Preschool

This is not a memoir. It's what I've been telling myself since I began writing this book, anyway.

"Remember, you're not writing a memoir."

What was I writing, then?

I don't know. A story, I suppose. Or maybe stories, in the plural. A recollection of bad and beautiful memories. A long-form complaint.

Why should it matter what I call this document? Who cares about conventions of genre? It's a fucking book, that's all. Call it whatever you want.

Now that it's finished, I've had to wonder why I'm so reticent to name it a memoir. If I'm being honest—and honesty is honestly what I value most about this little project—then it's basically because I don't like memoirs. They're generally overwrought, boring, and self-indulgent.

I'm not trying to be mean. That's just kind of how memoirs tend to be. Take this book, for example. It's all of those things. An author can only hope that their attempt at writing a memoir manages to also be something more. In the end, judgment belongs to the reader. Without the reader's validation, an author's work isn't much more than an arbitrary set of words.

You're supposed to have experienced something interesting or noteworthy in order to qualify as a memoirist. Or you're supposed to have done something unusual or remarkable. The idea is that you're somehow different from the average person. It's not a compelling metric. The line between spectacular and ordinary isn't always clear, and it seems to me that the task of a good writer is to avoid spectacle in order to transform ordinariness into something meaningful, or maybe to illustrate that ordinariness is in itself a meaningful condition, filled with joy and challenge. Our lives are taken up by interesting and noteworthy events, and we're constantly accomplishing the unusual and remarkable. Only some of us decide to record those events for public consumption. Even fewer get to do it as an exercise in highbrow writing. It requires a peculiar cachet. Therefore, what's considered worthy of a memoir, this distinctive category with its own vogue and etiquette, and in turn what's taken to be literary, are exactly the qualities that often make a memoirist seem aloof or pretentious.

I keep thinking about which parts of my life are worth discussing. I'm noteworthy because of a contentious and long-standing public controversy I experienced after getting terminated from a tenured academic position in 2014 (along with some preceding and subsequent controversies). But getting fired isn't really an accomplishment—I guess in some cases it can be—and I've spoken so much about it over the past eight years that a personal low point threatens to become my identity. I also worry that people have grown tired of the story.

The story is ongoing, though, because at base it's about the systematic repression of Palestinians and the precariousness of Native American and Indigenous Studies and those problems still haven't been solved. I was always a reluctant protagonist, which is perhaps why I continue to write about the situation and its aftermath, despite serious misgivings. And it never felt like my relationship with academe fully ended. Since I left the industry, I've experienced a nagging sense that something unexpected would happen and I'd end up back in a classroom, despite insisting to myself and others that it was totally over.

This ambivalence, too, is ordinary. Despite the attention I've enjoyed (or suffered, depending on its provenance), I still don't consider myself unusual. The great majority of us share a similar kind of insecurity: about money, about career, about health, about parenting, about inflation, about war, about sustenance, about ecology. Pervasive instability is our common burden. Our problems end up in the news, or they don't. Whatever the case, they're problems, all the same.

I'm uncomfortable when somebody prefaces a story of hardship with "of course it's nothing compared to what you've gone through," or some such qualification. I understand why it happens—it's an attempt at grace, but also a rhetorical convention common among activists and academics. Among those crowds, you can get a sharp rebuke if you veer beyond what's supposed to be your lane. I don't think it's an especially healthy way to interact, this tendency to isolate psychological and emotional troubles into discrete categories. Getting fired from a low-wage job is probably more onerous than getting fired from a university. Pain is pain, even without social capital attached to it. Nor do I want interlocutors to minimize their own adversity. We're brethren in struggle and I daresay a bad situation is even worse if nobody seems to care.

I suppose this unshakable need for fellowship is what compels people to consume a stranger's trauma as an artistic pastime, and why a genre so self-indulgent can also be remarkably intimate.

That's the thing. To make a memoir work, your self-indulgence has to be generous. You try to share material that might appeal to an audience's desire for relief in a hostile world. At that point, you're no longer a mere autobiographer; you've become a character in the reader's universe.

So, the successful memoir becomes a shared project, maybe even a project that does away with personal boundaries altogether. That's the only way we can avoid being mutually bored.

These are stories of a life inside, and beyond, academe.

And this book is our memoir. I hope it serves you well.

People are unjustly fired from jobs every day—every minute, probably, if we want to be pedantic about it. An ugly business, no doubt, at least whenever a person decides to quit viewing the world from management's perspective. It's a terrible thing to deprive another human being of income, but under capitalism, destitution is a natural condition. Industry produces surplus. Abundance makes waste. Civility requires privation. The need for poverty, in order to maximize industriousness, was a driving force of colonization in the United States. And so human beings come to exist as line items in the ghoulish metrics of production and unproductivity. Social value derives in large part from professional identity. Somebody needs to be indigent or expendable for the system to work. When I was fired from a tenured position in American Indian Studies at the University of Illinois in the summer of 2014, it wasn't some exceptional tragedy, but it was one of those occasional events that generates attention because of tabloid characteristics or acrimonious politics (in this case, both). I would recover by landing a job in Lebanon a year later, but that gig also ended badly—I wasn't technically fired but had a position for which I was selected eliminated because of outside interference. I left academe in 2017 and tried new things. I can't say whether or not they were successful because I don't care to validate banal algorithms of productivity.

An Honest Living

About halfway to the lot, a ribbon of cobalt rises on the horizon; when it's cloudy, a common occurrence in the mid-Atlantic, the darkness stays pure. The spectrum of color will change with the seasons, but now it is winter and the sun comes slowly, if it appears at all.

Upon arrival, I exit my car, leaving it unlocked, and strap on my hazel backpack which holds a bottle of tap water, a book (usually detective or spy fiction), lens cleaner, Imodium, a pen (I hate being anywhere without one), cough drops, hand sanitizer, two granola bars, and a banana. Garden mat and flashlight in hand, I begin my safety check, circling the vehicle for anything suspicious. Then I inspect rims, lug nuts, and tire tread before kneeling on the pavement to check the frame, slack adjusters, fuel tank, steering linkage, bushings, shock absorbers, brake lining, and a bunch of other doohickeys, a task that age and temperature make especially unpleasant. I open the door, examine the stairs and handrail, click the interior lights, unlock emergency hatches, and walk the aisle to make sure seats are properly bolted, exiting again into the cold morning, its cobalt replaced by the lucent bloom of dawn, where I check tire pressure, light covers, and compartments. After lifting the hood, I shine the flashlight on belts and engine parts and fluid tanks, finally removing the floppy dipstick to verify proper oil level. An elaborate brake test, three more walk-arounds, some additional prodding and dickering, and I'm done.

The lot is a colossal expanse of asphalt with yellow markings in diagonal patterns, circled by more spaces around the periphery. Despite regular bursts of sound and light, it's a lonely place filled with people but inconducive to conversation. Every now and again, I run into a colleague and exchange pleasantries. We rarely discuss management. It's a largely contented workforce.

"Have a good run," we say in closing. A good run can include any number of things, but mostly it means the delivery of uninjured children.

When I first climb aboard, the bus smells like an oncoming cold front. After the engine runs for a few minutes, it fills with the smoldering warmth of burning diesel. It will later reek of bubblegum and lunch meat.

I rev up and pull into rush hour, maneuvering through stoplights and turn lanes. The subdivisions on my route are sortable by income: garden-style condos, townhouses, single-family homes, and McMansions. In my area—the portion of the county where I'm assigned—most schools are mixed-income and ethnically diverse. Other districts are suburban, as imagined by Hollywood. I pick up bushels of children, some smiling, others nervous. I make sure they're seated before putting the transmission into drive. I'm still learning their names; they call me Mr. Steve.

Depending on the particulars of my route, I sometimes make it home for a smoke and a nap between shifts. Normally, I'm close enough to sneak back, but traffic in the DC region is unpredictable, tending toward intolerable. If escape is unlikely, I skim a book and doze in the driver's seat, nestled in a coat and hood when the exterior seeps through the capacious glass.

In the afternoon, I perform a shorter safety check and enjoy more small talk before pulling into a loading zone, hectic with the dither of freedom. Now the children are more enthusiastic and thus more prone to mischief. Every minute or two, I deposit mini hordes of cantankerous pupils into bustling subdivisions that will soon resume a quiet normalcy. I pull forward again. I stop a few blocks later. And on it goes until I've completed all three levels of secondary education.

That's me inside the panoramic windshield, a vagrant mercenary living a post-professorial life of interrupted motion.

■ ■ ■

Becoming a school bus driver wasn't random. I used to be a professor—I rushed my way into academe, in fact, landing on the tenure track (at a public regional university) straight out of grad school. I put in a good effort to make it happen, but the career felt manifest. My father taught physics at an HBCU in southern West Virginia and my earliest memories involve following him to work, chalk dust and textbooks intoxicating my emergent senses.

"Prof," he called me with booming approval, his breath warm with pistachio and nicotine. I earned the moniker by disappearing into my room for hours and validated it by becoming my father's unqualified research assistant. At some point during my childhood, the nickname became a decree. I went to college at seventeen knowing that I would never leave.

Twenty-two years later I got fired. Now I can't return.

We mainly think of job loss in economic terms. It's a reasonable focus; the suddenly unemployed must consider food and shelter in a society unempathetic to destitution. The destitute are terrific symbols of caution, which makes them a class to vehemently avoid. But we're also conditioned by jobs. They organize social relations. They influence mobility. They are essential far beyond utilitarian qualities.

I loved teaching, and often loved writing, but I had a hard go of things in academe. Three consecutive jobs ended in public controversy. I'm bothered by the (admittedly logical) inference that I courted drama or mistreated colleagues because of that controversy. In reality, I was only uncollegial in my reluctance to participate in the civic life of campus. That is, I vigorously minded my own business. My words weren't so reticent, however.

There are lots of stories from Virginia Tech, the University of Illinois, and the American University of Beirut [AUB], but they all end with the same lesson: for all its self-congratulation, the academy's loftiest mission is a fierce compulsion to eliminate any impediment to donations.

When I recall my hardest moments in academe, my thoughts invariably wander to AUB, perhaps because it was my last gig. As my contract wound down and the job market came up cold, every morning felt like the Friday of finals week. During this period, I finally understood the ugly possibilities of mendacity and alienation in spaces devoted to higher learning. A search committee had selected me for a directorship. Shortly after, some US Senators and AUB's reactionary donor class pressured the university's president to cancel the appointment. AUB has long been a site of soft power for the State Department. Platitudes about faculty governance and student leadership notwithstanding, universities inhibit democracy in ways that would please any thin-skinned despot. Despite vigorous protest from a small but spirited group of students and a smattering of bad press, AUB held firm. I left Beirut in August of 2017. The program I was hired to direct has since collapsed, though it maintains a five-million-dollar endowment.

The situation provided an occasion to confront the nagging trauma of infamy. Lots of people washed out of the news cycle can tell you that the upshot of recognition is disposability. Consumers want heroes, but heroism is contingent on the hero's willingness or ability to emblematize an audience's psychic and libidinal needs. In other words, adoration stipulates obedience, which produces a tenuous codependency. Conditions of support supersede the subject's control (and sometimes the subject's knowledge). The great paradox of public life is that leadership requires conformity.

Infamy never agreed with my disposition. I disliked the attention, which seemed to elicit vague expectations of reciprocity; I hated the rewards that come from reciting slogans and platitudes; I detested the tacit contract that I was supposed to be some kind of role model to people who proclaim mistrust of authority. After a while, I felt obliged to sabotage my fame. No media appearances. No networking. No phony relationships. No orchestrated controversies. No whiny monologues about being repressed. In short, none of the usual bullshit that goes into the making of a micro-celebrity. When a certain white liberal upbraided me for failing in my responsibilities as an "Arab American leader" (I had criticized one of Bernie Sanders's terrible opinions about Palestine), a return to pseudo-anonymity seemed to be the only viable response.

You hear ex-professors say it all the time, and I'll add to the chorus: despite nagging precariousness, there's something profoundly liberating about leaving academe, whereupon you're no longer obliged to give a shit about fashionable thinkers, network at the planet's most boring parties, or quantify self-worth for scurrilous committees (and whereupon you're free to ignore the latest same-old controversy), for even when you know at the time that the place is toxic, only after you exit (spiritually, not physically) and write an essay or read a novel or complete some other task without considering its relevance to the fascist gods of assessment, or its irrelevance to a gang of cynical senior colleagues, do you realize exactly how insidious and pervasive is the industry's culture of social control.

There are tragic elements to this adventure, sure. A political symbolism informs my academic career, and after months without work, my family suffered financial hardship. I didn't matriculate through the twenty-second grade in order to land a job that requires no college degree. Then again, neither did I attend so many years of college in order to be disabused of the notion that education is noble.

■ ■ ■

School buses are probably the most iconic symbol of American transit. Nearly everybody who grew up in the United States rode the bus as a child, even private school kids. It's rare to take a drive without seeing one. Itinerant yellow rectangles (though I always thought of them as orange) with black trim and amber lights, school buses are essential fauna in roadway ecology. Because of their ubiquity, few motorists notice them (as opposed to, say, the Oscar Mayer Wienermobile), but when stuck behind one, it's all a frustrated driver can see.

Most adults remember the school bus with mixed feelings. For some, it was a place of mischief and merriment, for others a site of anxiety. But everybody shares the experience of getting carted to boxy structures with brick exteriors and drab paint, where they sat in sterile cinder block rooms adorned ineffectually with cheery décor, and pledged allegiance to their own dispossession. The school bus is our erstwhile conveyance into good citizenship, blazing along with the promise of economic mobility.

The life of a driver, then, is surprisingly complex. The main task is simple—transport kids safely to and from school—but it involves various forms of delivery. We're supposed to facilitate access to education without considering its contribution to the oppression that informs our wages. The roads we traverse are monuments to automobile culture, spread across endless acreage in seemingly random, but brutally deliberate, patterns. This infrastructure emerged from racism, extraction, and accumulation, the bellwethers of civic pride, patterned and imprinted on an enervated, overburdened land. Every weekday morning, we spark the ignition, warm the engine, and put the spirit of colonialism into overdrive.

Yet the job induces primal expressions of love. School buses supersede their physical structure; they anchor a huge apparatus designed to guard the vulnerable. The machine is outfitted with lights and blinkers calculated to announce its presence. It is excessive on purpose. Nothing is more important than its cargo. SUVs, bicycles, eighteen-wheelers, ambulances, fire trucks—all abdicate their right of way when the stop sign and crossbar swing into the roadway. The school bus is one of the few institutions in the United States that protects the powerless from the depredations of commerce.

■ ■ ■

Reinvention is difficult in middle age, all the more so in relation to prestige and salary. Professing is more an avocation than a job, and so departing campus can be disorienting. My departure was incomplete until I became serious about a nonacademic career. It became final when I traded the hue of my collar. Incrementalism is good for think tank fodder and bureaucratic culture because it's a natural accoutrement to boredom. For people trying to overcome indifference or ennui, abruptness is a better approach.

People still call me "prof," but these days I dislike the title. I no longer see myself as an academic (and was always wary of pompous descriptors like "expert" or "public intellectual"). Forfeiting that title is more philosophical than practical. I no longer profess and therefore no longer assume the burden of professorial expectations. No more civility or nuance or dispassion or objectivity or whatever term they're using these days to impel obedience. It's as close to freedom as a prole can get in this self-deluded country, where the government legislates on behalf of the private sector and the private sector obliterates dissent on behalf of the government.

I wanted good work, honest work, the kind in mythologies of industriousness and humility, where humans with denim overalls deposit saline piety into the earth and die for rustic ideals of personal valor. I dreamed of coffee and tea and cassava raining down on the countryside. But I settled for health insurance. Like any person disavowed of reverence, I finally recognized the need to disappear into the system that destroyed me.

■ ■ ■

During the height of my infamy, I visited Toronto for a conference. I'd been traveling a lot and felt perpetually lightheaded. The line for passport control at Billy Bishop Airport was manageable. A couple of dozen yards into the lake-facing downtown, the airport is one of the few comfortable spots in North America for the economy class traveler. With about four parties between me and the window, I noticed that my pen was missing. My pockets and backpack came up empty.

"Pardon me," I said to the woman in front of me. "May I borrow your pen, please?"

She herded her two kids back into line. "I'm so sorry," she replied tartly, "I don't have one, either." I glanced at her freshly completed customs declaration card. "My children lost it," she explained.

I turned around but nobody was behind me. After pivoting back, I noticed the woman assessing me with a quizzical expression whose meaning was, by that point of my life, unmistakable. Before I could turn away again, out it came.

"Are you…*Steve*?"

I pursed my lips and nodded. She immediately launched into an indignant soliloquy about my plight that would have ended in pious assurance of support had the agent not called her to the window halfway through the performance.

I wasn't listening. Had she loaned me a pen, I could have written the speech for her. Instead, I seethed through a silent monologue: "No, I'm not fucking 'Steve.' I'm a careless son of a bitch who somewhere in or above this godforsaken continent, maybe at a stuffy boarding gate or in a cramped airline seat, lost a writing utensil that I normally guard with acute obsession. Because I'm human and humans do stupid shit. I'm not a disembodied mascot for public affectations of outrage. I'm just a crank who needs a goddamn pen."

When I reached the window, the agent looked unimpressed. "Listen, sir," I began, "I don't seem to have a pen. Can I use yours real quick?" He handed over a clear Bic with a black cap and pointed to the back of the room.

"Go over there. Fill out your card. Get back in line."

"Can I do it here? It'll just take a second."

"Go over there. Fill out your card. Get back in line."

"I promise it'll just be—"

"When you get back to the front of the line, be sure to return the pen."

I walked to the table and opened my passport. It took about a minute to complete the task. In the meantime, two planeloads had filled the queue beyond the final turnstile.

■ ■ ■

Academic jobs are notorious for long, convoluted hiring processes, but becoming a school bus driver, at least in the county where I work, isn't much easier. For an academic position, applicants submit a dossier (often packed with repetitive material), survive a screening interview (with a committee larded by ulterior motives), and visit the prospective employer for at least a day, during which they'll be tested and measured by dozens of gatekeepers, before negotiating a complex employment package and earning the governing board's rubber stamp, all of which can take over a year. Aspiring drivers attend an orientation, watch dozens of online videos, solicit moral references, pass a physical (including a drug screening), get a commercial learner's permit (a laborious process that requires extensive testing and hours at the DMV), finish classroom and road training (at least 200 hours), sit for various written exams (failure of a single exam can mean removal from the program), complete a half-day, commercial driver's license (CDL) test (which includes a daunting pre-trip bus check), and undertake at least two weeks of on-the-job training before finally showing up at the intake office to request a route that probably isn't available. Trainees are paid once they reach the classroom. I finished everything in about six months.

Before showing up to the classroom, numerous emails instructed us to arrive before 6:00 AM and wait to be buzzed in. They were particular about where to park and how to dress. I began to feel like the protagonist in a campy spy novel. The address led to a brown-brick office / warehouse combo in an industrial park filled with squat, rectangular buildings. The novel had taken a dystopian turn.

I parked my mom's 2006 Buick Lacrosse, its dashboard covered with Central American swag, and walked around the building, passing unmarked doors. The lot was filled with small trucks sporting the county seal. In front of the building, a sign, ten yards above one of the doors, read "SCHOOL BUS DRIVER TRAINING PROGRAM." I popped a lozenge into my mouth and pulled the handle. Inside were about two dozen people (nineteen, I'd later find out) waiting in a stairwell leading to another unmarked door. The trainees lined up in two rows, leaning against cinder block walls painted the color of uncooked biscuits. Nobody spoke, but we smiled and nodded our heads.

Soon a tall, owlish woman opened the door, latched it against the wall, and invited us in, offering everyone a personalized "good morning." Tired and wary, we wandered through dead-end corridors and finally found our classroom. The room was cheerier than the building, but still depressing. The heater worked and that was enough. Eight hexagonal desks were surrounded by disembodied bus parts: tires draped in snow chains, a simulated dashboard, fisheye mirrors, a simulated fuel tank, exhaust pipes, and drive shafts. It was like a mechanical, "stations of the cross" for bright-eyed Sunday school pupils.

Our instructor was setting up a PowerPoint presentation on a projector. I had met her months earlier at orientation, when prospective drivers formally submit their applications. She was in her mid-sixties, rail thin with a shock of frizzled blond hair above her forehead. Her name was Connie, and she was serious about her responsibilities, with a style that combined den mother and drill sergeant.

She asked us to fill in the empty nameplates adorning each table. What should have been a simple exercise quickly developed into farce. My "Steve" was uncomplicated only because it's my actual name. The guy across from me wrote "Tom." I tried not to be presumptuous, but he didn't look or sound like any Tom I've ever known. The guy at the next table didn't look or sound like a "Charles," either. One person wrote "J," skipping the "a" and the "y." Another wrote "E.J."

These names in fact proved fake when Connie took roll. Suddenly "E.J." (Eusebio, it turns out) was incomprehensible. "Tom" (Bountham) became an Indo-Chinese mystery. After Connie failed to pronounce "JungSook" half a dozen times, the woman she tried to identify added "(call Esther)" to her nameplate. Those who opted not to anglicize ended up with new names anyway: Mehdi was rechristened "Matty"; Susheela became "Sss…uh…Soo?"

Out of twenty trainees, seventeen were immigrants—and my parents are from other countries, so the room was brushing against ninety percent foreign. The all-American conveyance would be driven by surplus.

Connie was game, though. She'd sent hundreds of people from borderlands to school buses, and she intended to whip us into shape no matter how many sequential vowels or consonants she encountered. About an hour into the first day, she was reading from an HR document when she stopped short and glared at one of the tables. "Hong!" she bellowed. "*What* are you doing?" The guilty student looked up nervously from his smartphone. Everybody winced in sympathy at Hong's mistake (real name Shi-Hong, by the way). "You're on paid time. Cell phones aren't allowed."

"No, no," he pleaded. "I was just getting my social security number."

"You keep that thing on your phone?"

Hong looked confused, as if to politely ask, "Where else would it go?" He said, "Yes, on the phone, yes."

Connie feigned incredulity and continued the lesson. I was grateful for Shi-Hong's blunder; bursts of excitement were the only thing keeping me awake. Although I was a professor for nearly fifteen years, I never did well in school settings. Teaching was different. Time passes smoothly when managing a classroom, even on the rough days. Sitting in the audience, whether it's a seminar or training session or conference panel, has the effect of skin dripping down sallow cheekbones. Things that irritate the teacher are welcome from the student's point of view.

Since college, I've had a recurring nightmare about being forced through some absurd scenario into finishing high school. It's vivid to the point of tactility. The dank ambience of the old building, with its tawny walls and ossified classrooms, stays with me for the next day or two. I'm an adult among teenagers, terrified because I've skipped a class all year and report cards are coming. Sometimes I realize that completing the degree is unnecessary and announce to mom and dad my intention to quit. Usually, though, the dream ends inside school, before the salvation of cap and gown.

Halfway through my first day in the training center I realized that the nightmare will no longer be necessary. My subconscious wasn't processing the past, but preparing me for an unknown future, initiated by a departure from the constraints of education. Here was a different form of commencement. I suppose it's a common realization. The professional world doesn't offer escape from numbing consonance and enforced conformity; it rehearses those afflictions in more perilous environments. High school is forever. You have the chickenshits who talk big but never challenge authority; the alt-kids who jump at any chance to impress the cool crowd; the dickhead men (usually coaches) getting away with obvious abuse; the classmates prosecuting rules on behalf of administrators; the outcasts and losers everyone ridicules to enhance their own status, or avoids in order to preserve their spot in the social hierarchy. We don't matriculate through discrete existential increments; we reproduce the same dispossession across the entire accursed economy. To hell with reading, writing, and arithmetic; school is real-time preparation for the indignities of capitalism.

Connie evinced no mean-spiritedness, but she carried out the task of discipline with gusto. When we reached the section on appropriate handling of students, she launched into a diatribe about freaks and perverts, vowing to hunt down any among us and inflict corporeal harm. A man in the back of the room chuckled. Connie stopped mid-sentence and put her right fist on her hip, pointing her left finger in the air. "Excuse me?" Everybody turned around to see the man, who was smiling. "Why are you laughing . . . what's your name? Oscar?"

"I'm not sure," Oscar said in singsong English. "I just thought that was funny, you know?"

"What on God's green earth is funny about abusing children?"

Oscar wasn't ridiculing the abuse of children, but the person discussing the abuse of children as if she were narrating a Steven Seagal production. He was too gracious to point out the distinction. "Nothing funny," he shrugged.

Connie wasn't convinced. "Do you have children?" she demanded.

"I have a grandson in elementary school."

"How would you like it if some pervert did something to him?"

"I'd be very upset."

"Okay then," Connie declared triumphantly.

Oscar continued smiling, something we soon learned he did often. A few days into training, he began referring to me as "doc." The first time, I was taken aback. Did he know something about me? I decided he was being jocular, possibly riffing on my native English or my habit of reading novels during break. He didn't inquire about what brought me to the training center at middle age. None of us made such inquiries. Our group was friendly and supportive but adhered to an unspoken embargo on nosiness. None of us grew up dreaming of becoming a school bus driver. It didn't seem tactful to extract backstories. People drive for various reasons, but the profession is no stranger to hard luck. Everyone in my cohort was there either from boredom or deprivation: retirees looking for extra income, escapees from bureaucratic tedium, taxi/Uber subcontractors pursuing steadier employment, global drifters seeking relief in a brutal job market, inhabitants of a wealthy nation somehow in need of benefits.

The demographics of my cohort informed its restraint. We inquired about children, language, town of residence, and country of origin, but never about politics, religion, or ideology. Immigrants understand that social media algorithms and advertising categories are unstable. Plenty of Muslims support Trump; plenty of DREAMers want strong borders. People come to the United States for hundreds of reasons. Any one of us could have been an academic, dissident, grifter, politician, spy, prisoner, jailer, soldier, activist, peasant, or war criminal. The possibilities didn't matter. The moment we converged upon the training center, class became our shared priority.

■ ■ ■

The provost was desperate. I had ignored his emails for two days. His assistant got through by phone and implored me to come in for a meeting. The provost was eager to see me. That afternoon. No, it couldn't wait.

I climbed the hundred-plus stairs from my apartment to upper campus. I knew why I had been summoned: administration was pissy because a group of students had been agitating in response to the arbitrary cancellation of my appointment as director of American Studies. The group was small, but effective. It had upset management by connecting my situation to AUB's colonialist existence, a touchy subject at a lavish campus enclosed by barbed wire in an insolvent country suffering the hardship of US and Israeli aggression.

The provost greeted me effusively. It wasn't a gambit to put me at ease. Overwrought joviality was his thing. A tall, lanky man with the gravitas of a pogo stick, he had earned his job through the sort of obsequiousness that senior faculty love to confuse with merit. His office was spacious and dignified, with stone and hardwood flour- ishes, affecting the air of a midcentury secretariat in the tropics. The surroundings were jarringly discordant with their boobish occupant.

"Stee-fen!" he exclaimed after asking about my family, "there are strange things afoot on campus." It appeared that a few misguided students were yelling about some kind of injustice. I could see where the conversation was going, long before he got to the point, which was surprisingly forthright. He wanted me to quash the rebellion. I told him it wasn't mine to quash. You could quash it anyway, he noted (accurately). He made it clear that I would be rewarded if I named the troublemakers. The president, he declared, motioning toward the hallway, would put me "on his head," an expression that sounds less stupid in Arabic. "Put you on his head, Stee-fen!" he repeated, pointing at me with one index finger and tapping the other against his cranium. The offer wasn't especially appealing; the president stood at chin level, and I had serious doubts about his sense of balance.

The provost's proposition is standard operating procedure in the corporate university, though rarely so explicit. Assist in maintaining order and enjoy the compensation; disrupt progress and suffer a cascade of indignity. Campus governance is a masterpiece of pusillanimity. Upper administrators are happy to step in and maintain discipline when self-policing goes awry. Dozens of mechanisms, some imperceptible, combine to send the message that looking after the well-being of the wretched is a bad idea. Here, I had someone tossing away the pretense and informing me that cooperation might preserve my livelihood.

I told the provost I'd think it over. He looked pleased but unconvinced. I hurried down to my apartment and told my wife, Diana, about the meeting.

"What'll you do?" she asked.

"I ain't no fucking rat," I replied.

The students received no support from faculty, or from any demographic invested in the brand, eliminating the need for extortion. A few months later we packed up our home by the sea and moved into my brother-in-law's spare bedroom in Northern Virginia.

• • •

I was rarely nervous speaking in public, even when infamy provided large audiences. During that period, I was fighting for a cause, one indivisible from my career, and so I welcomed opportunities to lecture. Self-assurance gave way to nervousness after speaking became an occupation. Like any prestige economy, speechmaking is fraught with ego and betrayal. It requires self-promotion, networking, assertiveness, and all kinds of other things that I do poorly. People in the circuit are cognizant of the approaches and opinions that would limit their desirability and the size of their audiences. They also understand which demographics to ridicule and which to promote. Public discourse doesn't exist in a free market.

Academics, writers, and activists covet nothing more than speaking invitations, especially keynotes. Eminence isn't a neutral condition, but a commodity subject to intense competition. I can't count the times that I've seen someone crash a panel or presentation through artful politicking. A distinct subgenre exists of public intellectuals grousing about the horror of not being granted an audience. Repression as brand equity. It's a sad scene and a headache for anybody less interested in performance than upheaval. For oppressed communities, supposedly represented by prominent natives, the speaking-gig economy is just another form of dispossession.

Within a year of returning to the United States, I began ignoring or rejecting invitations. When the inquiries dried up, I didn't miss them. I no longer wanted to travel, especially by air. The worst elements of capitalism get crammed into pressurized fuselages: comfort is reserved for the high-end customer, who enjoys fast-track security, opulent lounges, and excessive legroom; everybody else is cargo. I always figured that an airplane is a good spot for revolution. It's likely to happen during the boarding process, when tired, cranky travelers who have been nagged and cajoled for hours file through business class on the way to economy and see a bunch of assholes chilling in spacious recliners, cocktails in hand.

Or they could sink into nineteen-inch-wide middle seats and concede that discomfort is the way of the world, that money justifies inequality, and with harder work they'll one day relax on the right side of the curtain. No number of adoring audiences, no accumulation of awards and honoraria, will influence their decision. They took too many bus trips to school as children.

Every now and again, while my family sleeps and I'm on the back porch enjoying the day's final cigarette, I think about my turn as a star speaker, memories that allow me to better appreciate the quiet of my surroundings. And while in pronounced moments of loneliness I do miss the company of the audience, the pleasure of applause and laughter, and the cathartic thrill of raging against injustice, the feeling is evanescent. The sobering immediacy of cold air on my fingertips and pressure in my thorax reminds me of both material and psychological limitations that render me unfit for prominence, being that I've become the kind of person content with the humdrum thrill of stopping traffic.

■ ■ ■

I wasn't nervous the first time I drove a school bus. I strapped the belt, adjusted my seat, and almost shifted into drive without pressing the brake. Nervousness would have been helpful.

I began on a transit bus, the goofy rectangular jalopies without a nose. They're tricky to steer because the tires sit behind the driver and the enormous windshield can produce a sense of vertigo. My trainer barked a string of instructions, but in my mind I was already cruising down the interstate. I never dreamed that metal and rubber could feel so natural.

Over the course of two weeks, I learned to make hairpin turns, merge onto highways, program a government gas pump, navigate country roads, cross railroad tracks, parallel park, avoid tree branches, and back into narrow spaces. Then I spent a few days on conventional buses, the ones with a hood in front and a huge overhang beyond the back tires. The final step was driving a supervised route, where I refined the art of deploying warning lights to impatient motorists. There were some dicey moments, but I kept the buses in one piece.

I thought of the training as a condensed university education. The diploma is a CDL, the bus driver equivalent to a doctoral student's comprehensive exams. This point isn't completely hyperbolic. I studied many hours for a CDL; the test itself took many hours longer. Getting to that point wasn't a certainty. By CDL time, my cohort had decreased from twenty to eleven. It's a terrible mistake to think of commercial drivers as unskilled.

Mostly, I was content with a new sense of purpose. A common feature of depression is being unable to imagine a decent future, one reason why insightful thinkers connect the condition to the scarcities of modernity and increasing recognition of a coming ecological catastrophe. I don't know that salvation can be found in labor, a notion that combines the most alienating elements of Christianity and capitalism, but I'm not disposed to pretend (anymore) that grace can be attained by discussing work in paid conversations.

■ ■ ■

My father isn't much of a talker, but when I was young, he occasionally spoke of honest work. It's a common trope around the world. Honest work emphasizes pride over salary. It's not measurable according to the value of labor, or the sale of labor to the overclass, but an abstract barometer of integrity. Movies and novels make heavy use of the motif: better to sling garbage or pick lettuce than join the mafia. The honest worker has no money but enjoys plenty of moral satisfaction.

Little ethical difference exists between legitimate business and the underworld. One group performs legal violence, but both rely on deceit and aggression to maintain an atmosphere conducive to profit. If anything, corporations surpass the brutality of cartels and black marketeers, or exist in league with them. Governments serve at the behest of corporations.

But even to a cynic, honest work has appeal. In a system that so adeptly makes livelihood contingent on obedience, few people can afford to be champions of the downtrodden. There's something comforting about the low stakes of an hourly wage, but there's no such thing as a thoughtless vocation. What the bosses call mindless labor in fact requires terrific exertion. I no longer have the energy to struggle through contradiction. It's easier to contemplate dispossession as an anonymous county employee.

Even as I complicate honest work, I'm aware of how indebted I am to the notion. It guided my exit from academe and my rejection of the pundit economy. I've always overvalued recalcitrance, a sensibility, as I understand it, that vigorously avoids situations that require ass-kissing, usually resulting in significant reputational harm. Since elementary school, I've searched for a space where I could conform to my surroundings without feeling unmoored from an inner sense of decency. That space, it turns out, is equivalent to the volume of a school bus.

I pitched honest living to my parents when I told them about the new job. Despite being aware of academe's ruthless memory, they hoped that I'd one day be a professor again. They probably still do. In a better world, my redemption would happen in the United States. I wanted to quell that expectation. "Even if Harvard offered me a job I'd say no," I proclaimed with earnest hyperbole.

They feigned support but didn't believe me. I understand why. It's hard to imagine coming of age in reverse. Hollywood doesn't make inspirational movies about struggling to overcome material comfort. We don't aspire to be part of the working class. Personal fulfillment occurs through economic uplift. We go from the outdoors to the office, from the ghetto to the high-rise, from the bar rail to the capital. That's the dream. To become a celebrity or a tycoon or, in humbler fantasies, a bureaucrat. But forward progress as material comfort is cultivated through the ubiquitous lie that upward mobility equals righteousness. Honest living is a nice story we tell ourselves to rationalize privation, but in the real world, money procures all the honesty we need.

For immigrants, these myths can be acute. I could see my parents struggling between a filial instinct to nurture and an abrupt recognition of their failure. My mom, a retired high school teacher, seemed interested in the logistics of transporting students, but my dad, the original professor, clenched his hands and stared across the table. It's the only time I've seen him avoid eye contact.

Parental despair is a well-worn theme, for good reason. The idea of a child's suffering, even in adulthood, has tremendous pathological appeal. But discovering a parent's grief is no less powerful. That sort of discovery is a critical feature of adulthood. Only after I witnessed my father's pained expression, his furtive anger, his shivering confusion, all of it poorly concealed by hard-boiled resolve, was I prepared to continue into an unknown world.

■ ■ ■

Connie only ran the first day of training, replaced by a succession of former drivers who were (like Connie) good teachers. They drilled us on the nuts and bolts of operating a bus, but also shared plenty of philosophical observations. Ours was a Socratic classroom.

More than anything, I appreciated the trainers' sense of proportion. They had to balance experiential wisdom with a rigid curriculum. They minimized certain lessons, surely aware that we'd find those lessons ridiculous.

I had read ahead in the two binders the county provided, which normally doubled my boredom. One unit filled me, simultaneously, with dread and excitement: communicating with students from diverse backgrounds. Three columns provided anthropological tidbits. For instance, Middle Easterners tend to be late, Hispanics (the manual's word) tend to be *really* late, and Asians aren't necessarily happy when they smile. Asians, however, are good at waiting in line, something to which Middle Easterners and Hispanics aren't predisposed. None of the groups can be trusted to mean what they say, but they all revere elders. We weren't privy to the nuances of African, European, Oceanic, or Indigenous cultures.

That lesson never came, though. The trainers didn't even bring it to our attention.

They did show a video about terrorism. Beginning with a slow-motion scene of a bus getting blown to smithereens, a voiceover giddily explained that the vehicles we drive are prime targets of evil. Its perpetrators come from any racial or religious group, the man (now on screen) stressed. The disclaimer increased in importance with each new image of ominous brown men with unruly beards. Amid foreboding music, viewers were regularly urged to call some high-tech hotline. After a few minutes, I realized that the pasty narrator wasn't a garden-variety expert; he was pitching a security company that he had founded, which compiles a database of suspicious activity based on anonymous tips. I suppose the film's budget for sacrificial vehicles and incendiary devices should have tipped us off that it wasn't the usual low-fi tutorial.

I glanced around the room, but nobody presented a visible reaction. We were more scared of the politics of terrorism than political terror. Common wisdom is that terrorism exists in part to create paranoia, but I don't think anyone feared a suicide bomber. More frightening was the possibility of being implicated in the government's security apparatus, which has transformed all residents into potential cops. Terrorism hasn't impeded our freedom; it illuminated all the reasons we are unfree. After the video ended, we waited in tense silence for the accompanying lesson, but the teacher walked into the room, flipped on the lights, and started discussing special-needs children.

The most consistent message throughout our training was the importance of students' well-being: greet them, provide some entertainment, watch for signs of trouble, bid them farewell. Driving isn't our only duty. We're part of the children's educational experience. Otherwise, the training would have been much shorter.

Well-being is predicated on functional machinery. Pre-trip inspection of the bus was by far the hardest part of the process. It requires a lot of memorization and practice. We spent many a dark morning splayed out on tattered yoga mats looking at the underside of a bus, sliding around on damp, freezing ground. I came home sore and cranky, my range of neck motion reduced by half, but proud that my old bones could still handle a bit of honest work. I tried to imagine some colleagues from the past contorting themselves beneath torsion bars and U-bolts, but it wasn't a satisfying exercise; I didn't want to think about those people in any position. Learning a new trade involves mastery of the exotic; leaving academe requires the craft of forgetting.

We can't put consciousness into formulas because we're too small for metonymy and too great for imitation. While it's able, the world produces incessant cycles of comfort and torment, affirmation and disappointment, reward and recrimination. I'm transported into the boundless ambition of childhood every time my son, who is in first grade, begs to join me at work. I dissuade the requests, but he's persistent. In the end I never say no. He knows a lot about how the bus operates and where it's supposed to stop. He even peeks underneath during pre-trip to make sure nothing is leaking. I've begun referring to him as my little professor.

I graduated with a Masters in English in 1999 from a regional-comprehensive in Southwest Virginia, fairly nondescript despite the lovely scenery, and immediately headed off to Oklahoma to pursue a doctorate in Native American Studies. I never really thought about doing anything else. At that point in my life, I was extremely driven, certain of both the probity of academe and my fitness in the industry. In fact, I didn't think of it as an industry at all. It was a simulation of adulthood, a monumental geography of patience and deliberation, a quixotic marvel of intellectual possibility. A benighted life. An exceptional living. Academe works much better under the spell of naïveté. Unfortunately, naïveté is a fleeting luxury for a great many people toiling in the pastoral regimes of higher education.

Career Training

"It's stupid," she kept repeating, growing more agitated each time she said it. I couldn't rightly disagree with her. It was pretty stupid, I supposed, although I was inclined to put it in the category of harmless stupidity.

I didn't say it out loud. She didn't seem amenable to nuance in that moment.

Before long, she revealed the source of her opinion: "Do they think everyone just has, like, money to spare? I swear to God, I hate all these rich little shits around here."

I could empathize. The stereotypical college set was never my thing. This was 1999, the first year I began using email and browsing the web. I was in my first semester as a doctoral student at the University of Oklahoma. I'd spent enough time on campuses by then to understand that they're filled with lively and (sometimes) even loving subcultures. But those places take time to find, and she was only in her first semester.

It made sense that she would be upset. She was hungry, and it felt cruel that an institution adorned with a million symbols of wealth would set up a huge grill in the middle of a quad in order to squeeze even more money from its students. She wasn't wrong about the low-key rudeness of the situation. It's something most people in the United States don't think twice about because we're so acclimated to the retail economy—making money is always the practical option—but cooking food in the middle of a public place and not offering it to the needy is fundamentally mean-spirited.

I thought it would be wise to distract her, but it was kind of hard to change the subject. The smell of grilled meat had seeped into every nook of the building.

I glanced at my watch. "Well, anyway, I'm really sorry, but it's time to head to class."

I didn't invite her to walk with me, but she stayed in her seat as I packed my things and then followed me out. I stopped at the food line.

"What are you doing?"

I shrugged. "I'm hungry, too."

Her eyes narrowed into the look of somebody about to suffer a tremendous betrayal. I didn't want my ruse to go too far. She was already correct to contemplate yelling at me.

"Don't worry, I have us both covered," I said.

She crossed her arms. "You don't have to."

"I know. Like I said, I'm hungry."

She gave me a humph but accepted the gesture.

We ate our hotdogs while walking across the rest of the lawn to the classroom building. It was a beautiful day, as early autumn often is on the southern plains. The cobalt sky had some filmy clouds around the edges, quickly burning away in the midday sun. A strong wind mitigated the overbearing heat.

The hotdogs were gone by the time we reached the building and both of us seemed satisfied. We hadn't solved the problem of hunger, but we had at least managed to eat. Sometimes that's the best you can do.

From that day on, she regularly visited my office hours. Her fiery hair was always unkempt, as if she made it a point to be vulgar. It seemed an appropriate fashion choice given the recurrent theme that campus was filled with losers and little shits. I listened attentively to these complaints. I wasn't devoid of sympathy, but I had an obligation to teach those losers and little shits and had already figured out that it's a bad idea to label your students as a teacher, the way you might have done as their peer.

We sometimes walked together from my office to the classroom. I left enough time for short detours to grab something to eat on the way. She always gave me the same glare before ordering. I made no production of it. We got our food and then ate while walking.

The semester ended and, all in all, I thought it had gone well. Everyone was still alive. Some had even improved as writers. At the beginning of the next term, I received my student evaluations. Back then they were a huge source of anxiety and anticipation, as opposed to later in my career when I didn't even read them. They were so momentous, so intimate, so critical to one's self-esteem. I would come to understand that they're nearly devoid of pedagogical merit and a source of even greater stress to untenured faculty, whose ability to remain employed often depends on them.

But at the time, they were like any other existential crisis. Bad reviews would mean rethinking my entire life. I opened the manila envelope with a mixture of fear and excitement. I looked at the Scantron results first. They showed a very good average, better than I had expected. That made it easier to flip through the written feedback. There were a few lukewarm and silly remarks, but on the whole the students had nice things to say.

With one exception. One set of comments was devastating. The reviewer had absolutely ripped me. I knew it was her. I recognized the language.

The good feelings immediately went away. "It's only one review," I kept telling myself. I was supposed to be above all that. Professional. Unemotional. Disinterested. A real scholar accepts criticism with dignity. (Whenever I see famous scholars falling out over petty disagreements on social media, I remind myself that I once believed in some ludicrous academic myths.) Anyway, none of that highfalutin stuff should have mattered: *all the other reviews were good.*

No amount of logic could dissolve the lump of dread in my stomach. The good feedback was meaningless. It would be the one dissenter who captured my attention. The review had uncomfortable reverberations: I hadn't simply failed as a teacher, but, with my overwrought reaction, I'd also failed the standards of my profession. It was made worse by the fact that I knew the reviewer's identity. If the author had been anonymous, I could have reasonably dismissed the review as an aberration. But the author wasn't random or disembodied. She was a real-life, honest-to-God student. She got good grades. We had an understanding. We had bonded.

I couldn't figure it out. Had I offended her? Did I say anything inappropriate? And then it came to me in a bittersweet epiphany: my student didn't hate me, per se; she simply recognized where I existed in the university's social ecosystem. Her contempt for the place was sincere. No amount of bonding could stop us from being class enemies.

■ ■ ■

I had chosen OU for its strength in Native American Studies and also because no elite program would accept me. They had little interest in an undistinguished applicant from a little-known regional-comprehensive in Southwest Virginia, eager to put Native America in conversation with Palestine.

I was an unlikely candidate for an intellectual career. I had grown up in a declining coal and railroad town that straddled the border of Virginia and West Virginia. My dad was a physics professor at Bluefield State College and my mom (until that point a homemaker) began working as a Spanish teacher when I was ten. She had no particular desire to go to work. The local school district needed somebody to teach Spanish and convinced her to do it. There weren't more than a dozen Spanish speakers in town. Señora Salaita was the area's most famous Mexican, despite being from Central America.

She had made use of the language before. When I was a kid, she sometimes translated for the federal court in Beckley, West Virginia. I loved hearing her stories about the convicts and their behavior in the courtroom. Most were there for some kind of drug charge and mom felt like they were getting a bad rap. It made no sense to me. This was the height of Nancy Reagan's *Just Say No* campaign and we schoolchildren were made to understand that drugs were the evilest thing on earth. Nancy wasn't so forthcoming about her husband's role in the trade. Mom was well aware of the discrepancy.

One day mom came home from court feeling sad. She explained to me that the defendant she was translating for—"just a child, a nice girl"—had muttered something to her about the judge. The judge caught the exchange and demanded to know what the defendant had said. Mom tried to play dumb, but the judge got mad and ordered mom to translate. When she stalled, the judge threatened her with contempt. Mom watered down the comment, but the damage was already done.

"The thing is," mom explained sadly, "the girl was right. God forgive me, but the judge *was* un gran pendejo."

I think she was happy to get into teaching. My mom is Palestinian, but she grew up in Managua and she's a whiz at Spanish. Whatever facility I have for language comes from her. I took her Spanish 1 class in middle school—a terrible idea, and everyone knew it, but there was no other choice—and even in eighth grade I could see that she was a knowledgeable and passionate grammarian. To this day, I love asking about various dialects and geographical conventions and then listening to her explanations.

It's not that I lacked solid examples for a teaching career; I appeared to lack the talent. It turned out to be mostly a lack of initiative, and once I settled into college as an English major, I transformed quickly into a diligent student. I had always loved to read and it felt like cheating to get a degree for something I would have been doing, anyway. My behavior had straightened out, but my attitude was the same as ever. I just needed some focus. In time, I began to appreciate the psychic benefits of directing my insolence at centers of power.

By graduation, I was a 4.0 student, after having spent five semesters in the mid-twos. I liked my professors and classmates and was offered a full scholarship, with stipend, so I stayed on for a master's degree knowing that I would continue on to a PhD. With no pedigree and middling GRE scores, I wasn't in the best position. By the late 1990s, the humanities job market was already bleak and competition for grad school slots was brutal. I was thrilled to be heading to Oklahoma.

I had no hang-ups about going to another state school. I wanted to take interesting classes and be in contact with different national communities. Oklahoma fit the bill. I know it sounds stupid or arrogant, or both, but I never doubted that I would end up with a job. I didn't want to rely on branding or institutional reputation. I intended to publish like hell in order to make up for my other shortcomings. The first part of the plan worked: I had a nice little list of peer-reviewed articles when I went into the job market and had published six books by the time I was thirty-five. But that couldn't overcome the biggest shortcoming of all: being Palestinian.

It was a hell of an impediment to academic success, even for those who fancied themselves apolitical. I was ambitious, but also practical: nobody who talked a lot about Palestine was getting hired with the measly accomplishments of your standard company man. I needed to far surpass average. But becoming exceptional is its own impediment. It means you haven't adequately conformed, a serious problem in academe.

I remember that on various interviews, at least one Zionist, who had nothing to do with the search, would come poking around, asking passive-aggressive (and often illegal) questions: do you travel often to the Middle East?; where are your parents from?; do you drink?; what got you interested in literature?

Sometimes the questions were loaded with implicit racism (more than usual, anyway): how do you intend to handle Jewish students? what are your thoughts on the peace process? do you support suicide bombing?

As soon as this peculiar kind of nosy poker showed up, I knew I wasn't getting the job.

People might act surprised or skeptical when Palestinians tell horror stories of life in academe, but, if anything, we undersell the horror because even bowdlerized versions of Zionist suppression are unbelievable. Think of it this way: you exist in a space that prides itself on pushing boundaries, on challenging orthodoxy, but your existence is wholly contingent on a byzantine ability to render yourself nonexistent. You're an embodied boundary of the orthodox, the point at which the status quo allows dissent before reasserting its dominion. In short, you are, merely by existing, a biopolitical weapon.

I was aware of these problems by the time I began my doctoral program, although I didn't really have the vocabulary to describe them. In those days, I thought of English as a pro-Palestine field, owing to the influence of Edward Said. I wasn't completely wrong. I just didn't know at the time how easy it is to be both pro-Palestine and anti-Palestinian, or anti-Zionist as a selective branding mechanism.

It's hard to remember a time when this stuff wasn't at the back of my mind. The bad experiences started in elementary school. Each month, I remember another example of brazen Orientalism or racial hostility.

I wasn't naïve about the problem of anti-Arab racism; I was naïve about the open-mindedness of academe.

■ ■ ■

After arriving in Norman, I spent the days exploring campus and its surroundings. There wasn't much to see, just the standard stuff in a medium-sized college town: dive bars, apparel stores, and seedy housing. I had expected the flatness of Oklahoma to bother me after a lifetime in Appalachia, but I immediately took to the open spaces. Across the road from my apartment—a two-bedroom that rented for $400, including utilities—was a large park with a long thin duck pond. The grass always had the same ochre color no matter the season. Mature trees never seemed fully verdant. They constantly left filigrees of dead leaves on the ground.

One day after grad-student orientation ended, I wandered around Gittinger Hall, the English Department building. (It's now called Lin Hall and houses a physics research lab. The university razed the apartment complex that I lived in, Parkview, a few years after I graduated.) I hadn't met any of the faculty I intended to work with. I knew that Alan Velie would be my dissertation advisor, but I had no idea what he looked like and was a bit intimidated to meet him. I had no information about the man to be wary of; I was simply insecure.

Alan was something of a legend in Native American Studies. He had his detractors, in part because he was white (Jewish, to be more specific), and in part because he could be intractable. He came to OU in the sixties as a classicist, teaching courses on the Bible and Shake-speare. At the end of the decade, amid campus upheavals around the country demanding ethnic studies, a group of Native students approached Alan, asking him to offer a section on American Indian literature. He obliged, and a few years later became an important critic in the field.

The protagonist of that story is quintessentially Alan. It was easy to picture him agreeing to teach the class without outward enthusiasm and then preparing diligently on the students' behalf.

Wandering around Gittinger that afternoon, I came across Alan's office on the third floor. The décor around his nameplate was lively. I was reading some flyers when suddenly the door opened. I jumped backward, but Alan barely seemed to notice me, this strange, bearded kid lingering outside his office. He glanced at me without changing his expression (slightly bothered, but not enough to make a show of it), gave a short nod, and went on his way, leaving me to keep reading his door if that's what I wanted to do.

I had expected somebody upright and imperious, but Alan was short, with rectangular glasses and shocks of unkempt white hair on either side of his head. He looked like a Hollywood scientist or maybe a children's librarian. He was walking with a cane, the result, I would learn later, of a recent hip surgery. Alan had the mien of a seasoned grouch, but his gentle demeanor was unmistakable.

I was mortified and wanted to run into the nearest classroom. Alan made it around the corner and I dashed off in the opposite direction. Surely, I worried, he'd remember the awkward moment when I introduced myself as his newest doctoral student.

If he did remember the encounter—and experience would tell me that Alan wasn't one to forget anything worthwhile—then he deemed it unworthy of conversation. His usual method was to ask me what I intended to do with a particular topic or chapter and then listen patiently while I fumbled through an explanation, achieving none of the erudition I tried to exhibit. He'd then shrug and tell me that it sounded fine, go on and get to it. Alan gave a wide berth to anyone he perceived as a self-starter. It worked out perfectly for me, full of vim and ambition.

Best of all, Alan didn't give two shits about my politics. He wasn't that kind of guy. Only once in all the time I spent with him did he solicit my views on Palestine.

"What do you think?" he asked without a hint of reproach in his tone, "about the solution proposed at Madrid?"

The 1991 Madrid Conference formalized the land-for-peace arrangement, alternately known as the two-state solution, which has since fallen out of favor among many Palestinian activists and politicians. In the early 2000s it was still the mainstream view among the left-liberal diplomatic set and a normal point of reference for students and scholars interested in Palestine. Alan was curious as to why I rejected that framework.

I explained that persistent Israeli settlement of the West Bank had rendered a viable Palestinian state impossible and expressed general skepticism about the diplomatic protocols led by the United States and Europe. I also dropped my inhibitions and declared that all of Palestine is occupied, and the right of return nonnegotiable.

"Okay," he shrugged and that was the end of it.

I'm sure that Alan had plenty of opinions about the issues I was covering in my dissertation—he was extremely well-read and intelligent—but he wanted me to sort them out. If I needed criticism, he provided it; otherwise, he had no interest in sketching a rubric for me to fill with conventional ideas. This unspoken emphasis on freedom would become a huge part of my pedagogical approach. I hated the idea of guiding students toward an outcome that fit my preferences. It's common in graduate school for advisors to impose self-serving strictures, and if direct coercion proves ineffective then suggestiveness usually does the trick. In this sense, a lot of students function as laborers alienated from the products that they create.

There's no way to put forward universal criteria for good advising. It depends on the advisor's ability (or willingness) to perceive an individual student's particular abilities and then prioritize the qualities favorable to intellectual labor. If the advisor has no ulterior motive, and the student isn't a jackass, then good work can usually emerge from the relationship.

Before the start of my third year, Robert Warrior, who had been denied tenure at Stanford in what was widely perceived to be a prejudiced decision, joined the OU faculty. He was (and remains) a giant in American Indian Studies and I immediately asked him to serve on my committee.

In many ways, Robert was Alan's opposite, but he too expected a certain level of self-motivation. An Osage, he had published notable work on Native nonfiction (including Osage naturalist and novelist John Joseph Matthews), along with journalism and scholarship on the American Indian Movement, Native literary criticism, and liberation theology. A former student of Edward Said, Robert had spent time in Palestine when he was younger.

A fair amount of people expressed skepticism about my topic, wary in particular of anything to do with Palestine, but Robert championed the project and urged me to write through the doubt. He had explored the idea of Palestine as a promised land in a famous essay, "Canaanites, Cowboys, and Indians," and was eager to see others develop analyses of internationalism in Native American and Indigenous Studies.

Whereas Alan would usually shrug and, in his gruff manner, say "keep going," Robert was an extremely attentive reader. I was downright scared to put work in his hands, not because he was a mean or ungenerous reader, but because he read so carefully and compassionately. The work needed to be good, and if it wasn't, Robert had a way of getting the point across to devastating effect, without being an asshole. It's much easier to disappoint people that you don't respect.

My dissertation would later become a book, and the comparison of Native America and Palestine grew into an accepted pursuit among scholars and activists. The legibility of the topic is what got me hired by the University of Illinois ten years later, into a program that Robert was chairing. When my firing became a national story, Robert's program suffered tremendous opprobrium, along with Native American and Indigenous Studies more generally. I always balked at the idea that the event was a singular injustice featuring a lone protagonist (or antagonist, depending on your point of view). The discourses that emerged from the controversy acted as a referendum on the utility of Native Studies, which illustrated a stubborn disapproval of Indigenous nationalism among the liberal elite, in and beyond academe. It was dismaying for the American Indian Studies faculty at Illinois, along with advocates of Indigenous liberation around the world.

Through it all, Robert acted as both friend and advocate. At the beginning of the ordeal, when the sense of shock was still acute, we would chat on the phone, thinking through ways that I could begin my job. Neither of us considered letting it go. Our shared attitude was simple: I had been hired and it was time to begin.

Once, I apologized for creating so much headache; Robert calmly replied that responsibility for the problem belongs solely to the university. It would be the beginning of the long, difficult process of not blaming myself for the depredations of the managerial class. It's not as easy as it sounds. Grad students are carefully trained to disidentify with the less powerful party to any conflict, even when they're the less powerful party in question.

The aftermath of the imbroglio would be messy. The newspapers don't normally tell readers about the personal upheavals that accompany most of the controversies they cover. So it was with this one. Nearly all the American Indian Studies' faculty that taught at UIUC in 2014 now work elsewhere. Robert ended up at the University of Kansas, closer to the Osage homeland. Vicente Diaz, a dear friend with a generous soul, moved up to the University of Minnesota, along with his wife, Christina Tatiano DeLisle. Jodi Byrd went to Cornell.

I've heard so many stories of grad students abandoned or screwed over by their advisors that, despite some pretty intense trouble, I consider myself lucky. To have had a positive experience studying for my doctorate automatically makes me better off than many of my peers. I've made friendships that will outlast even the most optimistic fantasies of what I could have been in academe.

The victims of such trouble get to experience a different sort of education, with an off-the-record curriculum, but one arguably more consequential than the formal variety. I look back to those days in Gittinger Hall as a kind of prehistory, a moment in which an innocuous set of ideals about the lives of the mind was still intact. I didn't know it was unusual for graduate mentorship to create a sense of asylum from the ugly forces within the industry. It just happened that way. I don't know if it could have happened anywhere else, but I was determined to recreate the paradigm if I ever ascended to a position of authority.

■ ■ ■

Those of us with teaching assistantships were responsible for two sections of composition each semester. We got no course releases for dissertation prep or anything like that, but the pay was enough to survive in Norman. At OU, the curriculum for first-year composition was tightly controlled by faculty in the rhetoric and writing program and their advanced grad students. We taught specific units with uniform readings and assignments. There was some wiggle room, especially with style of instruction, but basically we were teaching toward a distinct model of assessment.

I had no problem with it and don't remember much discontent among my cohort. It can be difficult taking a full-time graduate course load while teaching two sections of composition, but I rarely felt overwhelmed. There was plenty of spare time, or maybe I perceived certain responsibilities to be extracurricular because I didn't view them as work. I was living a longtime dream.

● ● ●

I was twenty-three when I arrived in Norman, not much older than my hungry student. I had taught composition for two years while getting my master's degree, so I wasn't entirely a newbie at OU. I think back to my mentality and maturity at twenty-one and realize that it was pretty much malpractice to put me in charge of a classroom. Then again, I know plenty of old hands who are shitty instructors, so I suppose this stuff isn't scientific.

Most people audacious enough to do graduate school in the humanities probably fancy themselves unusual, and in this sense I was perfectly ordinary. I got along well with my cohort and with people on campus in general, but I never felt like a typical grad student. Younger grad students drank a lot and spent many hours a week socializing. I was never into the bar or house party scene. I had a lot of acquaintances and very few friends.

I devoted most of my time to writing. Part of it was practical: I knew that I needed a substantial CV to have any hope of landing a job. Mostly, though, I wanted to be a writer. I liked doing it more than other things. Whenever anyone compliments me on my writing—a lovely thing to hear—I want to explain that I have no special aptitude. The hours I've spent at it are incalculable. It's a craft that requires tons of practice and it's easy for me to tell who has put in significant time learning how to do it well. These writers are easy to spot because they're so rare.

I'd always been timid and a bit jumpy around other people, but writing was a comfortable environment for both work and pleasure. It was my primary social life and anyone who thinks that books don't count, that they're the opposite of a social life, has a very small imagination, or an overinflated view of their friends.

When I was a boy, my mom would force me to go outside because I liked to hole up in my room with a little stack of books. When I grew up, there was nobody to usher me anywhere and so I could be reclusive to my heart's content.

My all-time favorite place to read was on the school bus. (Don't worry, I only did it when parked.) I kept a novel tucked into the side panel and extracted it whenever possible: in the dark mornings after I'd finished my pre-trip inspection and waited for the air tanks to fill; in the quiet moments before kids filed out of school; sitting in line to top off the gas. Hell, sometimes I pulled out a book when I caught the beginning of what I knew to be a very long stoplight. There was something unbelievably cozy about being in the seat, a tight enclosure, reading by the dim overhead light and feeling the floor heater blow against my legs. It was the perfect job in terms of finding alone time. When I heard the *psssh* of compressed air from beneath the bus, I would return the book to the side panel, flip off the overhead light, and get on my way.

The best time to read was during morning layover. Normal schedules involve three runs in the morning and three in the afternoon. In either shift, most drivers have a break of between fifteen and thirty-five minutes. The trick of the layover is to find a good spot to park the bus. On one of my routes, a bunch of us used an empty church parking lot. That was nice. We could walk laps or stand around and chat, without worrying about traffic.

When I first started as a driver, I had a hell of a time finding a decent place to put my bus. My layover was exactly half an hour and the area I drove in was pretty dense, with no viable street parking. I raised this concern with one of my supervisors and she went out with me one morning to scout for some possibilities. Until that point, I spent half of my break occupying a Metrobus stop and the other half driving in a circle until my counterpart showed up to scoop or drop passengers. As I approached the starting point of my next run, the supervisor pointed to an empty streetside a hundred yards from my first stop, with more than enough room to put a bus.

"What's wrong with that?"

"There's a no parking sign."

"Honey, they ain't gonna give you a ticket."

From then on, I had the best layover spot in the world. Next to the street was a grassy area and a small patch of woods. I could hang out there, just out of sight of the nearby townhouse complex. There was hardly any foot traffic. I would park, release the air from the brake tanks, and rest against a large tree trunk for around twenty minutes. If it was raining, I stepped into the woods. When I heard kids walking to the stop, I knew it was time to climb back into the seat. No matter what was happening—an upcoming garage trip, a midday run, unruly children—I've never felt so relaxed with a book and a cigarette.

One morning, I opened the bus doors and saw a pile of fresh dog crap. "Gotta remember that" I said to myself as I stepped over it and headed to my usual spot. I didn't remember it, of course, and wondered what the hell was on the floor of my bus when my right foot wouldn't get any traction. The smell tipped me off. I lost a great pair of shoes that day.

I was reading at least two novels a week during this time. I didn't need anything too complex or avant-garde, but bad writing bores me, even in a good story, so it couldn't be shlock, either. I was into noir, detective stuff, a bit of mystery. I mowed through Graham Greene's oeuvre and a bunch of the lost classics published by the *New York Review of Books*. I wasn't in the mood for anything pretentious or self-consciously "ethnic." I didn't care about historical significance or curricular possibilities. I no longer had the obligation to think of books as professional objects. They were just books, something to consume for insight or enjoyment, it didn't matter which. And just like that, all the debates I'd spent half a lifetime on—abstruse rhetoric about authorial positionalities and textual ambivalence, which seemed momentous and even metamorphic at the time—didn't mean shit to me anymore. A book exists. You pick it up if something about it attracts you—perhaps the cover or the color scheme or the font or the name of the author. You decide that the jacket description is suitable. You read it when you have the time. You either hate or like it, or else make your way through it out of boredom or obligation. You put a review online or talk about it with a friend. Or you don't think much about it ever again. Then you find a new book to read. Having participated in the ritual, you've become a literary theorist, whether or not you're aware of it.

I sometimes tried to imagine what it would be like teaching whatever book I had just finished. It occurred to me, first and foremost, that the stuff I was reading wouldn't really be usable in the classroom based on my areas of specialization. I didn't teach British literature or modernism, so Greene was out (and would have been dubious for other reasons, as well). There certainly wasn't much chance to assign Raymond Chandler or Agatha Christie. What would we talk about, anyway? Phillip Marlowe is an interesting character, but he isn't exactly Ahab. Even Christie hated Hercule Poirot, so I doubt students would want to spend quality time with him. You could do some interesting stuff around communism with Dashiell Hammett, but why not Brecht if that's the direction you want to go? I guess in my mind it seemed adequate to have a chat about fun, interesting books. Teaching literature was never so simple, though. What we teach has to be *Important* and the criteria we use to determine *Importance* is often deeply conventional. Thus the need for theory to sort these complexities (or to complexify simplicities).

I could afford to be romantic, beneath my large shade tree at the edge of Annandale, Virginia, where I was perfectly content and also profoundly lonely. All I could really remember was that teaching provided a wonderful reading community and it was rewarding to view a text from the perspective of twenty different critics. My bus driving colleagues knew me as the guy with his face always in a book, which aroused some curiosity. But most everyone left me alone with my habit. Their indifference was a good thing because it's horribly annoying to be asked what you're reading—many people read in public precisely to avoid small talk—and I didn't want anyone to know that I was a disgraced former professor. I wasn't ashamed of my past but recognized that it was a great conversation topic which would have wrecked my anonymity. Anyway, I had long been conditioned to avoid discussing Palestine on the job, and being surrounded by immigrants from the Global South didn't wipe away the reluctance.

So, I had no students or colleagues with whom to congregate around the frustration and joy of reading. That was an activity reserved for more formal environs. Sometimes, I acknowledged while stretched out on the grass with my bus parked in front of me, I missed the classroom. Goddamn did I miss it.

• • •

When I began at Oklahoma, I had already cultivated a reclusive mentality. I wasn't constantly alone, though. I simply prioritized work over socializing. (Healthier labor relations would leave plenty of time for both.) I ran with a medium-sized circle of students, mostly from the Middle East or of Arab background. I always thought it wise to step outside of one's department for recreation and merriment, lest you get stuck in a cult-like atmosphere, to which graduate programs are already susceptible.

My predilections being what they were, I refused to carry a cell phone or to answer the landline in my apartment. The university, which owned the building, put an old phone in there and paid the bill, else I wouldn't have hooked up a line.

The apartment had a small, rectangular living area with a couch and armchair facing the front window and a kitchen table behind them, next to a built-in cabinet. My computer covered the table. It was a noisy desktop of late-nineties vintage with an enormous monitor shaped like a packing crate. It blocked most of my view of the front window. I kept a space to the right of the keyboard for coffee and a space to the left for an ashtray.

I'd be in the chair for hours and if the phone rang, I usually ignored it. One night, I let the phone ring and a few moments later checked my voicemail. A friend had screamed: "ANSWER YOUR FUCKING PHONE I'M DRIVING BY YOUR APARTMENT RIGHT NOW AND I CAN SEE YOUR HEAD STICKING UP ABOVE THE GODDAMN MONITOR!"

With friends, it's fine to act like a fool. Professional spaces are more tenuous. Don't get me wrong, you're definitely allowed to act like a fool in professional spaces, but the foolishness needs to comply with a certain etiquette. Ghosting colleagues and skipping social functions to smoke weed are a no-no. The professionals prefer foolishness of a loutish or belligerent variety, not the kind that makes life more peaceful.

Among friends, my aloofness was a source of frustrated amusement and an excuse to poke fun at me. Professional colleagues didn't view it as a quirk or a preference, though. My inability to socialize—unwillingness, really, for I was capable of doing it if I had wanted to—was a legitimate concern. They had a departmental culture to worry about. And I had promotions to secure. It did neither side any good if I insisted on making my existence in the department clumsy or standoffish.

In grad school, this stuff didn't matter much, but I wasn't long on my first job, at a regional-comprehensive in southern Wisconsin, before recognizing that "fit" was a critical (if vaguely articulated) part of the job.

You start noticing certain looks and glances that are damn near imperceptible but deeply momentous in what they aim to express: a quick purse of the lips; a slow-motion nod; a suggestive arch of the eyebrow. You become literate in the esoteric vocabularies of departmental and campus cultures: we believe in this or that Catholic ideal; we carry ourselves like an officially licensed mascot; we practice a specific brand of courage and honor. We're *Hokies*, goddammit. *Sooners. Highlanders. Phoenix. Fighting Illini.* We never give up. We take one for the team. We transcribe our identities in Latin.

Wisconsin wasn't so bad. I was twenty-seven when I arrived, eager to please and with barely a cynical synapse in my crystal-clear brain. Everyone rightly saw me as a kid. And they liked that I would do a lot of grunt work without complaint. Besides, the faculty lived across a hundred-mile range, so there wasn't a ton of interaction off campus. Most people chose a group of friends according to ideology or convenience and stuck to it.

Virginia Tech, my second job, was different. Almost everyone lived in or near Blacksburg, small even for a college town. The place had a real *rah-rah* spirit. English wasn't simply a department filled with workers of unequal status—it was a *community*. We weren't supposed to pay mind to things that divide us; we were on a collective mission to bring close reading to the world. And so you couldn't keep out of the way. I grew accustomed to colleagues passive-aggressively noting that I wasn't at such and such soiree or making it clear that the end of semester department party wasn't actually optional. Decline somebody's dinner invitation and watch that fucker vote down your tenure bid. After all, nobody wants an asshole on the faculty.

Only after I was done with academe—or I suppose after academe was done with me—could I fully appreciate the interplay of competing impulses in the making of a college professor. So many grad students and young scholars present themselves as tormented, and for good reason: they're overworked and exploited, and at the end of it all there's only a small chance that they'll earn a living in their areas of expertise. But the condition extends to people who should have long ago outgrown early-career angst: senior scholars, administrators, and visiting faculty, many famous or highly decorated.

I have my suspicions but do know it's not a great idea to do amateur psychoanalysis in writing. (We all do it in our own minds, obviously.) Let me then attempt to raise my discourse to the level of theory: we're all fucked up to some degree because it's impossible to reconcile the ideals of academe with its reality. The only happy people are the abusers, the bullies, and the sexual predators, and they're all inherently miserable. Many of us enter the field with dreams of a meaningful existence, of *making a difference*, and are then systematically ground down by the social and economic hardships of the profession.

Under these conditions, the ideological cliquishness within the profession begins to make sense. It's helped along by a power structure that rightly sees the self-professed scholar-activist as unthreatening. Certain truisms and devotions prevail because they arise from an insidious pressure to conform. If every professor that you know seems to have the same take on Venezuela or Ukraine or China—the take that just so happens to align with State Department boilerplate—then it's not a funny coincidence. Those professors auditioned and were consequently selected for the task, just as they now select the younger generation in order to maintain a uniformity of thought that suits their class interests.

I had no idea how ideologically stunted I was until leaving the profession. Everything I took to be common wisdom was in fact a painstaking ritual of complaisance. How eager I was to discourse about faraway places, about the proper way to run a government, about how the natives should conduct an insurrection. A lot of academics are filled with unacknowledged messianism that looks grotesque once you learn to recognize it. They won't support any old revolution, any slapdash movement for Indigenous sovereignty, any third-rate, anti-imperialist in the Global South. They have *standards*. And whose interests do those reverent standards end up serving? Why, that's entirely the wrong question.

■ ■ ■

The two years I spent in Beirut were eventful. I arrived with a good amount of fanfare and often ran into someone I knew while walking the streets of Hamra. There's a lot of poverty in Lebanon, along with a lot of refugees, so the romantic tributes to this remarkable country can be difficult to stomach. Nevertheless, there's no denying that Beirut is a magical city, one of those rare places that manages to breed nostalgia in the present.

I remember during my first semester at AUB, in the fall of 2015, *Bernie fever* gripped the left in the United States (and beyond). I was lukewarm about his candidacy, being that I have limited interest in electoral politics. Nevertheless, I observed the hoopla and occasionally joined the endless discussions about the Democratic Party primary that dominated social media. I was content to mainly keep out of it.

With time, I became unwilling to overlook what I viewed as Sanders' subpar positions around Palestine. I was less patient about the propensity of his supporters to delegitimize Palestine as an issue of concern. My feeling, which will never change, is that no oppressed people should be expected to defer their liberation. If Palestinian liberation doesn't figure into an electoral platform lauded as revolutionary, then the platform is demanding exactly that kind of deferral.

I wrote an essay explaining this point of view and immediately found myself in the middle of an imbroglio. The essay was unpopular among everyone from progressives to communists (according to self-description). I got called the usual names—purist, wrecker, ultraleftist, useful idiot—and gave back a little attitude in return. All in all, an unpleasant few days, but pretty typical of electoral discourses, which rarely manage to be coherent. (To be fair, neither do the actual elections.)

A week or so after the essay was published and the ruckus had died down, I was meeting a group of colleagues for dinner in Hamra. We gathered at the bottom of Jeanne d'Arc Street and made our way into the compact neighborhood. Not a block into the journey, somebody demanded to know why I wasn't supporting Bernie. (I detested that first-name basis shit. "Bernie." As if he's your kindly old uncle and not a powerful man who votes on military appropriations.) I explained that my position wasn't really about supporting or rejecting Sanders, but about what becomes of the least powerful among us when we tacitly ratify their dispossession.

"Okay, but you're not voting for him, right?" somebody else piped up.

"That's kind of beside the point."

But it wasn't. The group peppered me with questions about my voting strategy. I'm thinking of something other than voting strategy, I protested.

And suddenly it occurred to me: I was speaking an entirely alien political language. My point just didn't register. The idea of not voting was inconceivable. Worse, it was irresponsible and suspicious. Voting was the lodestar, the totality of civic life. Imagining other possibilities, even in the abstract, didn't enter the calculus.

As the chatter moved on to less acrimonious topics, I kept silent. Soon I became rather angry, because there was a plain reality I couldn't let go of: their political language, not mine, was out of place in Beirut. Had the discussion taken place in the United States, I would have been aggravated, no doubt, but in Beirut the conversation felt like an affront to the entire Middle East. Here we had a group of Western professors, earning a very nice living in an Arab country—at a university that graduated hundreds of anti-Zionist revolutionaries, no less—who felt the need to castigate a Palestinian for refusing to abide any form of Zionism, no matter how progressive it tried to make itself sound. Something about the whole scene felt profoundly unsettling. Perhaps it was the realization that my group was mimicking the logic of colonization, zealously in thrall to a stubborn variety of US exceptionalism.

It was the same among the entire leftist academic class, besides (maybe) the minority for whom Sanders was a bit too spicy. The usual rituals of conformity and recrimination ceased to be implicit or unspoken; suddenly the intellectual vanguard was dogpiling anyone impudent enough to dissent. Adhering to the logic of electoralism is an unspoken prerequisite for an academic or media career. Reject it and opportunities quickly dry up. Electoralism is less a political litmus test than a character audition. When an insurgency arises, the liberal elite needs to know that you'll have a pragmatic reaction, that you're available to lecture the riffraff about more responsible forms of protest. They need to know that you're inclined to conformity, that you care about access and upward mobility, that US exceptionalism has adequately colonized your intuition, that you're capable of radicalism only in theory. Declining to support Bernie Sanders—or, put more accurately, refusing to abandon Palestine to a politician's benefit—was the worst career move I've ever made.

■ ■ ■

I would think about those moments when alone on the bus, in between routes or going to the garage. It's hard to imagine asking a school bus driver whom they're voting for, and practically impossible to imagine demanding that information. You might get a halting answer or a shrug or a funny look. In any case, the question would seem suspicious. A demand would be downright rude. Perhaps the suspicion is an effect of Trump, but I figure it was always that way. Why would a bus driver be fretting about yet another election in the first place? They've got a whole lot of other shit to worry about.

■ ■ ■

These academic customs are slowly going away. Members of the learned professions have long bemoaned their receding influence, but it usually came across as an empty complaint. Social media has given them new life as influencers, while also illustrating the low regard with which they're perceived by much of the reading public. They haven't handled this discovery very well.

Over the years I've noticed a common rhetorical tic on Twitter and other social media: the professor as laughingstock. I'm not speaking of the public intellectual, exactly, which is a more abstruse category, but actual professors. There's a difference. The public intellectual needn't be affiliated with a university and the professor needn't necessarily seek publicity. The very category of "professor," as a distinctive economic class, has a new identity in the social media age.

Take the kind of response you might see when a professor tweets something asinine or obsequious (no matter how incisive the professor imagines the point to be): "Harvard professor, opinion discarded"; "lol political science"; "University of Chicago in bio." I grant that such comments are immature, but I won't concede that they're unproductive. In fact, I think they represent an important counterforce to the self-appointed authority of professors in the metropole.

The trite responses to professorial *hot takes* are, at base, an attempt to ensure that social media won't become lost to credentialism. It's probably too late—was probably always too late—but that doesn't wipe away the underlying sensibility. Users with little to no power are upholding an ideal that is meaningful beyond the internet. They're saying that a social media platform is optimally democratic and therefore shouldn't reproduce corporate media strictures in which luminaries carry water for centers of power. In fact, on social media, credentials are largely viewed in the negative. The Ivies come in for the most ridicule; users are more lenient with individuals from less elite institutions. (Then again, it tends to be the bigshots who share the most asinine and obsequious takes.) I like the sensibility, despite its excesses, because it shows that without the ability to coerce, many luminaries are baldly mediocre. Affiliation, more than ingenuity, accounts for their appeal. In fact, service to power facilitated the affiliation in the first place. Within the hermetic environs of campus, the famous professor wields significant influence. On Twitter, he's just another ninny with a dumb opinion.

■ ■ ■

Smart-aleck online commentors are capable of imparting useful lessons, as is any category of skeptic. I think back to my years in graduate school with a vague sense of shame because I believed so much mythology about the scholar's benighted role in society. It's easy to view myself as a victim, but I was also gullible. The gullibility wasn't impartial because in the end those beliefs were self-serving. I wanted to believe them. Believing them made me vital, seminal, exceptional. Believing them benefitted me materially. A bit of skepticism, now so pithily expressed in acronyms, would have done me a lot of good.

As it happens, I gave up on academe because I believed the mythologies. I still wanted some version of an honest living but knew I couldn't find it on campus. And if I looked too hard, I would make myself unwelcome.

That's what happens when intellectual life exists in a controlled economy. You go along and they allow you to eat, grudgingly or enthusiastically, depending on your attitude.

And sometimes you just have to accept what the bosses feed you. But that doesn't mean you're obliged to like them.

■ ■ ■

Political controversies notwithstanding, I've lived a pretty clean life. I've never had a one-night stand, never stepped out on my wife, never solicited a prostitute, never bedded a student. I don't get drunk. I don't gamble. I don't find addiction to be edgy or fascinating. I'm more timid than prurient, but I've also never been attracted to the idea of casual intimacy. My vice is nicotine, which I've imbibed on-and-off (mostly on) for over thirty years. I like to smoke weed, too, which I had to give up when I started driving a bus. But even here I do it as a ritual of aloneness. None of that vape or gravity bong weirdness. Just a spliff that I roll by hand and enjoy on the back patio, after my son has gone to bed.

All this is to say I'm nothing of the hero or villain ascribed by infamy. Those are internet character arcs. There's nothing inherently valiant about driving a bus and pissing off the ruling class certainly isn't villainous behavior. I'm an unremarkable person who avidly expresses opinions about a subject known to generate controversy.

It's difficult to write a memoir on this premise, but stories worth reading sometimes arise from dullness, and I'm hoping this might be one of those occasions. I have no bawdiness to offer, but I've managed to live an eventful life, nonetheless. The best thing I can say for myself is that I excel in the craft of recalcitrance.

Really, that's all I have to talk about. Nearly everything I write is some variation of the theme. It provided me with a research topic. It motivated me to beat the odds and land a job on the tenure track. It got me expunged from US academe. And it drove me onto a school bus.

I didn't have my pre-career checklist in order until my career was over. The stages of grad school aren't merely coursework, comprehensive exams, dissertation, and job interview training (if your department is kind enough to provide it); those stages exist in a byzantine cartography of self-promotion and ass-kissing. You have to master the informal demands of higher education in order to matriculate. That means knowing when to invoke the wretched as a branding opportunity, and when to dump them in service of upward mobility. Both actions can happen in the same day—in the same public lecture or Twitter thread, even.

But it doesn't have to be like that.

Nobody makes us conform to ghoulish paradigms of success. At the end of the day, it's a decision we make. Upward mobility is merely a form of compensation; it doesn't justify anything.

There's not much more to say about it, so I'll take leave of you for the moment with a dash of unsolicited advice:

> With every particle of your mind, with every atom of your soul, resist the idea (into which you'll be insidiously socialized) that compassion for the persecuted and dispossessed is unprofessional, that failing to satisfy relevant centers of power is a career move worse than death.

And that's really all I can offer you. It also happens to be everything I have.

My lawsuit against the University of Illinois dragged on for over a year. When the university filed a motion to dismiss, the judge, a Reagan appointee, wrote a scathing opinion affirming that I had in fact been fired and that the university's rationale for the decision required a defense in court. Despite some severe skepticism about organs of the state as a site of redress, the affirmation felt wonderful. I knew that if nothing else, the suit had set an important legal precedent in academic hiring, namely that trustees don't have a right to interfere in faculty governance and that social media comments are considered extracurricular speech. Other aspects of the process were less rewarding. I won't rehash all the considerations that go into a civil proceeding but suffice it to say that it requires an ability (or at least a willingness) to organize contradictory inclinations into a coherent strategy. I settled the suit at the end of 2015, to the disappointment of many observers. Contrary to popular belief, however, the suit wasn't actually a slam dunk. It would have taken years to litigate, at tremendous expense. I likely would have won in the end, but there was also a chance that I would lose and end up owing the university money. Or I could have won with only nominal compensation. Such are the peculiarities of the legal system in the United States. (Public controversies always contain intricacies unavailable or unknown to spectators.) There was a critical lesson learned in the process that I hope isn't lost to memory, one that any person who has challenged a center of power well understands: class unity among the economic and political elite is inviolable. It exists not simply as a method, but as a principle, and that principle is ironclad. The ruling class and its quislings will never provide an antecedent that empowers the less urbane elements of society. So it was with the University of Illinois and its political chaperones. The university was willing to spend unlimited funds on lawyers and PR firms but refused to concede more than a pittance to the victims of an obvious injustice. Part of the calculation in settling the suit was that I had secured a permanent position at the American University of Beirut, which would have mitigated any damages. AUB's treachery was therefore doubly harmful. But a greater part of the calculation was sentimental: I had gotten the favorable court ruling; I had earned the unanimous support of professional associations; I had won the battle of public opinion; and thus I wanted nothing to do with ghouls and scoundrels any longer.

Left-Rights

Driving is a poor way to learn about a place. Walking enables a person to discern the minutia of lawn design, roadside detritus, home disrepair, fraying utilities, and domesticated wildlife. It adjusts the perception of civilized habitats. Bicyclists become familiar with grading, pavement conditions, wind patterns, shoulder clearances, and shortcuts inaccessible to cars. Both modes of transport provide an intimacy with physical surroundings precluded by the speed and structure of a vehicle.

Driving, however, represents a place as it was meant to be seen by those who designed it. There are exceptions, of course, but urban development in the United States is largely based on two kinds of supremacy: white and automotive. Blight can disappear with some creative highway planning. Strip malls and expressways maintain segregation. Gates and tollways restrict geography according to desirability, itself a byproduct of race and money. Certain neighborhoods look uninviting to the downtrodden, based on the kind of serenity that suggests police diligence.

The vehicle a person drives also influences perception. I operate a school bus, for example, and since I began a familiar environment has become overwhelming. I know trash day by zip code; areas where residents suck at parallel parking; left turn lanes likely to produce congestion; corners where pedestrians cross on red; stoplights that take forever to change; and dozens of wayward signs and telephone poles.

Cul-de-sacs are a nightmare. Most are too tight for the bus to navigate without backing up (a no-no); all of them interrupt momentum. Going around the block (the normal way to correct missed turns) is a rare solution in the neighborhoods of Northern Virginia, which are filled with asphalt circles. Getting lost is a source of serious stress. Because of the inability to freely navigate, as in a car, the design flaws of suburbia are glaring—if they're flaws in the first place. After all, DC itself is encircled by a highway. It's easier to drive *around* the city than *into* the city.

■ ■ ■

What is suburbia's most emblematic feature? Picket fences? Basketball hoops? Tract houses? Strip malls? Stoplights? Man-made ponds? Lawn jockeys?

What about the cul-de-sac? It has to be in the top five, right? The cul-de-sac isn't an object or edifice, per se, a thing we readily visualize, but it aptly represents the peculiar class structure of US society. It's an architectural dud that kills the joy of walking and wastes acreage for the sole purpose of cramming oversized houses onto limited space, while maintaining illusions of privacy. Under capitalism, even circles manage to foster disconnection.

The cul-de-sac isn't isolated, though. It illuminates the triumph of automobiles, with all the global violence their preeminence requires. It affects property values, a petite bourgeoisie obsession, and thus facilitates the disbursement of compatriots into discrete subdivisions. It nurtures fantasies of safety and serenity, paving over the terror of a less disciplined world.

I dread running into one, but I see them everywhere, these oblate monuments to repetition. On my first day driving without supervision, I missed the turn into a school, something the passengers happily pointed out, and set about to double back. I took the next left and ran square into a cul-de-sac—an RV taking up around a quarter of the space.

The kids giggled as I muttered sanitized obscenities. Backing up to the main road was risky; it was too busy, and visibility would be limited. A U-turn was out of the question, thanks to the RV. I knew that I'd soon panic, so I decided to just move the bus wherever I could find space. I inched the nose onto a driveway and then slowly reversed until the RV filled most of my mirrors, repeating the process a few feet at a time. Five minutes later I had completed a nifty nine-point turn. Sweat poured into my eyebrows as I raced away.

The loading zone at school (normally crowded, I'd later learn) was empty. "Sorry I made you late," I called out. The passengers reassured me that they weren't upset. My misfortune was their pleasure, a situation that would be repeated a week later.

I know some people desire cul-de-sacs and others never think about them, but I hate the goddamn things. They make me feel like I'm cruising through Thomas Friedman's brain. And they disconnect neighbors in ways that make cooperation and comradeship virtually impossible. Those disconnects are evident from the air. Check out residential development from a window seat during takeoff or landing. You'll see cul-de-sacs spread across the landscape like grape lollipops, their houses separated by mere yards but, for all intents and purposes, in different cities.

The cul-de-sac happens when a society scorns public space, or at least when private development stands in for universal social preference. It's an epiphenomenon of the profit motive, fancied by consumers made to imagine a world with endless resources, enough, anyway, to manipulate unlimited space into middle-class utopias. The cul-de-sac isn't simply an ideal; it's an impossibility. The kind of security it promises can only exist by maintaining precarity in neighboring environs.

Although cul-de-sacs seem random, there's a logic to their preponderance. They isolate communities into classed enclaves, manifesting a colonialist myth that development is the epitome of progress, each flattened sphere its own exceptional world. Home buyers cite safety as a major attraction. What does it tell us about a society that the absence of intersections is considered desirable? More than anything, it says that people who can afford single-family homes by commuting to technocratic jobs desire protection from the same machines that created their fantasies.

Sooner or later, though, a flustered bus driver will barge into the space with a passel of rambunctious children and no idea how to get the hell out of there.

■ ■ ■

One of my routes goes to a working-class apartment complex populated by immigrants. Its parking lot is filled with food trucks and work vans. I have two stops at the complex, where I deposit around seventy-five elementary schoolchildren. Then I have a final stop elsewhere with two students, after which, barring unforeseen problems, I'm done for the day. The final stop is at the stem of a cul-de-sac, a mile by road from the apartment complex, but no more than a few soccer fields in actual distance.

I'm jolted by the proximity of the cul-de-sac to the complex, despite the rupture created by artful placement of park land and commercial property. Juxtaposition of poor and rich neighborhoods is supposed to be a feature of cities in the Global South, but it's not uncommon in the United States (it's long been a feature of a rapidly gentrifying DC, for example). Urban planners in the United States are adept at designing infrastructure that compartmentalizes people, while maintaining illusions of equal access. They don't tell you that access is contingent on unequal opportunity.

The working-class apartment complex offers exhilarating contradictions. It is worn down, with piles of trash bags outside of overflowing dumpsters, but it also possesses an energy absent from manicured subdivisions with single-family homes. Street life exists in the apartment complex: adults congregate on stoops to chat in multiple languages; children scurry across receding green spaces; everywhere one hears the reassuring noise of music, laughter, argument. Whatever its problems, the complex has achieved the status of a community. The cul-de-sac, on the other hand, is an empty gesture of civic obligation.

Despite bureaucratic attempts to standardize Northern Virginia, the covert capital of the US Empire, interesting activity insists on bursting through the planning. Arlington, where DC sends its high-rises, is a lost cause, and will only grow more yuppified with the arrival of Amazon. Alexandria, which once boasted a robust Black population, is on a comparable trajectory. The edge city of Tyson's Corner is a study in futuristic banality, and the business district around Dulles Airport has all the charm of a boarding gate.

But amid a landscape of spies, lobbyists, consultants, and politicians, alien life exists in ribbons of unrefined habitation. Here, notions of community govern social conduct, where residents decide that not every square inch of their neighborhood will be demarcated by HOA legalese and microscopic claims of possession. Hell, sometimes children even spontaneously knock on doors and ask their friends to come outside.

These spaces, crisscrossing a programmatic county, highlight the irrepressible human desire for kinship and vivacity. Governments and institutions are capable of controlling life down to its mundane details, but no ruling formation has ever been clever enough to legislate humanity into dullness.

■ ■ ■

In my industry's parlance, route sheets are called *left-rights*. A route sheet sounds simple, but so do Ikea assembly instructions. Its main purpose is to guide substitute drivers. Some are outdated, others incorrect. At times, typescript is crossed out and replaced with illegible scribbles. And left-rights don't merely tell a driver where to go, but also where to stop for pick-ups and drop-offs (along with confidential medical information and lists of students who must be released into adult care). It's common for drivers to pass a stop without locating the cross street.

These are problems with the route sheet, which say nothing of the problems with the road. Northern Virginia is fairly well marked, but not all intersections have signage, and not all signage is adequate. Street signs can be in terrible spots, covered by foliage or wind-damaged—if they're actually pointing in the right direction at all.

GPS isn't allowed. It appears to be a silly rule for such a prosperous, high-tech region, but the reasoning is solid. We have to worry about clearance and aren't allowed to turn left across two or more lanes unless at a stoplight. If there's an algorithm that accounts for these factors, then management either hasn't discovered it or is content to roll with tradition.

This isn't to say we don't use technology. The central office can track the movement of every bus (*bureaucrats* can use GPS) and knows when a driver opens or closes the door. Every bus also has multiple cameras, something that occurs to me whenever I'm tempted to pick my nose or sing along to "Little Red Corvette."

"Why don't they just call them *directions?*" Diana asked when I was learning the system.

It's a good question, one for which I still have no answer. I suppose *directions* lacks pizazz or isn't adequately colloquial. If administrators want to shoot for maximal accuracy, "left-rights" should be called "folios of clusterfuck."

Reducing navigation to two directions can imply that driving is a mechanical occupation, easy to understand. Whenever I get lost (a regular occurrence during my first month), I have a hard time explaining how it happened and why it was so disconcerting (just as, when I was a professor, I had a hard time explaining that I worked more than six hours a week).

"Don't you have directions?" family members inquire.

"Well, yes." Thus out of words, I endure the pitying stares.

Imagine making your way through unfamiliar subdivisions designed by people concerned less with functionality than profit, in heavy traffic (for school transportation roughly coincides with rush hour), holding sheets of paper covered by dense (and sometimes inaccurate) data that you're only allowed to view at a complete stop. Now imagine doing it at the helm of a thirty-eight-foot vehicle with protruding side mirrors, a vicious tail swing, and dozens of children playing back-seat driver. Only people who have never actually worked believe that any type of actual work is easy.

Left-rights promise simplicity, but they're lying. The terms connote harmonious opposition, a kind of spectral interplay, but this too is a lie. Like all binaries, left and right derive energy from one another, and they don't always lead to expected destinations. We also encounter circles, crooks, and curves, some leading to gridlock, others to unmarked interchanges.

∎ ∎ ∎

She's large for a kindergartener, in both stature and spirit. Ruddy and overfed, she asserted her claim to the front of the bus on my very first day. With volume and defiance, she crowds anybody impudent enough to annoy her.

It's easy to picture a future of drunken fights and financial struggle. In so many ways, she already reminds me of an adult. I'm certain that she's already seen the ugly side of adulthood in her short five years. One afternoon, she held up the bus by refusing to sit down. Four teachers had to carry her off the bus. Another afternoon, she wouldn't stop kicking the child who serves as a safety patrol. She didn't return to the bus for a week.

I liked her from the moment she glared at me and declared that her new assigned seat would be wherever she felt like sitting.

That seat ended up being behind me, where she holds forth with endless knock-knock jokes. Many are funny. She has an agile mind. Every day without incident, I stop her on the way out and tell her I'm proud of her good behavior.

One day the kids were fighting as they boarded. Two of them shouted "fea!" in the background (fea is Spanish for ugly). I turned around to quell the dispute and saw her squeezed against the wall, arms crossed, eyes puffy.

I sprang from my seat and grabbed the intercom mic. "Listen to me!" The appeal blared through the speakers with minor distortion. "Nobody on this bus is ugly. Nobody." The kids had never seen me upset and stared with a mixture of shock and curiosity.

It's remarkable, the amount of backstory that can occupy a flash of temper. In the second it took to get on my feet, I remembered dozens of scenes from my childhood school bus. A younger, darker me, with crooked teeth, unruly hair, and goofy eyeglasses, playing the timeless role of an unsightly foreign kid, surrounded by derisive normalcy.

"You're all beautiful. Every single one of you. Do you hear me?" I finished, my voice breaking, before slamming the mic against its latch. It hung crookedly until I parked for the evening.

The next day, she ambled up to me and stood erect, her mouth only a few inches from my eyes.

"Hey bus driver!" she roared. "I HATE YOU."

"You hate me? Why do you hate me?"

"Because I do."

Then she smiled and nestled her face against my chest.

■ ■ ■

I got into an accident during my second week on the job. It was a minor event, resulting in moderate damage to a car and none to the bus. Three elementary students were on board; nothing happened to them. I barely noticed the accident when it happened, but it has provided a lasting memory.

I was maneuvering the bus through a tight space between cars parked on either side of a residential street. A minivan came from the opposite direction and interjected itself into the space, which was too narrow for both of us. I veered right and was almost in the clear when I heard a hollow popping sound, similar to a cork exiting a champagne bottle. I had knocked off a side mirror from an Altima parked at the front of the line.

For a second, I contemplated driving away, but I quickly scuttled the thought. The students' expressions indicated that they had noticed the collision. I couldn't pretend it didn't happen. This wasn't like swiping a twig or scraping a curb. Part of a car was in the middle of the street.

"Hold on, I think I hit something," I announced, pulling the bus to the side. I was shaking. I couldn't believe it. Only a few days into my new career and I had committed the second worst error (running over a person is first). I gathered myself and radioed in the accident. A few minutes later, a supervisor turned up, followed by a cop. The supervisor (preppy for a bus driver) was businesslike and distant. The cop was friendly. I trusted neither of them.

It took around half an hour to make a statement and complete the paperwork. Meanwhile, another driver came and scooped my students. After assessing the damage with the cop and supervisor—I had popped the car's side mirror and scratched its front left fender—I scurried back to the bus, prepared to drive it across the county to the garage.

Now alone, I lost command of my demeanor. A succession of traumas—the stress of unemployment, the fallout of defamation, the abrupt uprooting from Beirut, the physical toll of too many twelve-hour days, the months without medical insurance, the bracing loneliness of my pre-dawn commute, the fear of losing this job and again having to find a new vocation—flooded my brain, a staccato montage of images feeding my cortex an antidote to serotonin. I let out something akin to a howl as my head quivered against the seatback.

In subsequent weeks I slowly rebuilt my confidence, though caution is anathema to my disposition. The three students on board during the accident helped. They raved about how awesome it was seeing the car mirror fly into the air and bragged to students who board later in the route about all the excitement. As per kid custom, their attention soon drifted elsewhere. I wasn't so fortunate; my employer follows a rigorous protocol in the aftermath of accidents. I'd have to attend various meetings and a three-hour driver improvement course.

A week after the accident, the supervisor who processed the scene called on the radio. He needed to reinsert the cartridge that records footage from the bus. When he arrived at my window, his expression seemed off. I couldn't place it. Some combination of pitying and bemused. Only after he finished the task did I realize that the folks who reviewed the tape almost certainly saw me crying.

■ ■ ■

The driver improvement course was, as advertised, an education. I expected warmed-over tutorials and platitudes about road awareness, but the three hours proved more interesting. The instructor asked each of us—about twenty-four in total, including someone from my training cohort—to diagram our accident on a whiteboard, describe what had happened, explain how the accident could have been prevented, and impart a few lessons from the experience. I volunteered to go first—not to suck up or to set a good example, but because I planned on dozing off (I'm adept at napping from a sitting position) and didn't want to be interrupted. Drawing a bunch of rectangles (cars), arrows (traffic patterns), squiggly arcs (roads), and a black circle (the doomed car mirror), I told my story, finishing with an admission of guilt and a promise to do better. I did it all wrong. Nearly everyone else offered a learned, detailed analysis of why the accident wasn't their fault, argued with the instructor who fruitlessly recited policies from the driver's manual and scrutinized the whiteboard like sweaty lawyers during a televised trial. It was so riveting I forgot about the nap.

■ ■ ■

"Hey bus driver!"

I peek in the rearview mirror (the "student mirror," it's technically called) to see three little heads poking above the seatback like smiling meercats. My second day has aroused their curiosity. I catch their eyes in the mirror. "Yesss?"

"What's your name?"

"Bus."

Their smiles disappear, replaced by perplexity. Kindergarten humor is paradoxical: clever but earnest, boundless but specific. They don't yet comprehend irony, one reason why they're more likeable than adults who pretend to comprehend irony. Even when kindergarten humor is mean, it never uses racism or sexism as a motif.

"Your name is bus?"

"That's right."

"What's your last name?"

"Driver."

"Your name is Bus Driver?"

"Bus Driver. Yep."

They begin to realize I'm bullshitting, but they expect sincerity from grown-ups. One of them finally pipes up: "Nuh-uh! What's your real name?"

I laugh. They join in, jumping up and down.

"My real name is Steve." They accept the answer.

"How old are you?"

"Guess."

"153."

"*One hundred and fifty-three?* What's the matter with you? 153? I'm only 143, thank you very much." They agree that the new number is more reasonable.

"Why don't you have any hair?"

"Because I'm bald."

"What's bald?"

"Not having any hair."

"What's that on your ear?"

"A mole."

"What's a mole?"

"That thing on my ear."

Now all the kindergartners want to participate in the interrogation.

"Do you have a girlfriend?"

"Yes." They are scandalized. Whoops and squeals bounce around the metal interior.

"Who?" The question comes from many directions.

"My wife." More scandal.

"Do you have a crush on her?"

"Very much, yes." By this point even the fifth graders are hooting.

I arrive at the school and swing into the unloading zone feeling strangely accomplished, having completed the most honest interview of my entire career.

. . .

Since switching from professor to school bus driver, I've learned all kinds of new stuff. One thing towers above all others: developers should never, ever, under any circumstances, be allowed to name streets or subdivisions. (Most of them should be chucked into prison, but we'll let it go for now.) Cultured people make fun of Las Vegas for its ersatz monuments, but Vegas is true to its gaudy character; suburbs are the real wasteland of ridiculous simulation.

One mixed-use development around here is called Fair Lakes. It has no lakes, though, only artificial, murky ponds with scrimpy fountains that by any decent standard aren't fair, but fucking ugly.

Or the Mosaic District. It's not a district. It's a few acres of new urbanist tedium with chain stores and pretentious restaurants. One could spend hours walking in circles around Anthropologie and Williams-Sonoma without finding a single tile. The place is a source of special offense because my father is from Madaba, Jordan, famous for its intricate and ancient mosaics.

And, good lord, the street names. The highly abridged list below could, if completed, take up half the cloud storage in the Dulles Corridor:

Pinecrest Vista: Pines, sure, but no crest and certainly no vista.

Thames / Parliament / Cromwell / Victoria / Derby / Piccadilly: All in a subdivision clearly designed by somebody with an Anglophile fetish.

Mount Corcoran Place: California is 2,500 miles away, fellas.

Lighthouse Lane: Where streetlamps ensure that SUVs don't crash into mailboxes.

Barnstable Court: Why not name a street in Virginia after a random town in Massachusetts?

Halcyon Lane: It has *two* cul-de-sacs.

Sunny Hill Court: It's no Sesame Street, but it's trying.

Golden Falcon Street: For fans of Dashiell Hammett.

Ad Hoc Road: Designed by a committee of grumpy professors.

Stirrup Cup Lane: Shit like this happens when drunken aristocrats get naming rights.

Autumn Ridge Circle: No ridges; otherwise, accurate three months a year.

Wheatland Farms Court: Beneath this asphalt something useful once existed.

Chase Commons Drive: Every square foot is private property.

Fountainhead Street: I have no idea what it looks like; government vehicles aren't allowed.

MacBeth / Titania / Falstaff / Oberon / Ariel / Capulet / Horatio: See, English majors can make money, too.

Nantucket Court: Wait, which state are we in?

Assembly Drive: Gather there and find out how quickly white people like to call the cops.

Lake Normandy Lane: Not even Normandy has a Lake Normandy.

Sideburn Road: Now we're talking.

I'm being picky, no doubt, but these naming conventions, consistent across an entire region, reveal something about people who design the suburbs. We can learn a few things about their inhabitants, as well, but it's not so easy to understand habitation through abstract critique.

From the perspective of a suburban ruling class—in Northern Virginia's case, often coterminous with a national elite—the goal is to produce veneers of idyll. Planners and developers promote visions of urbanity and grandeur by invoking nostalgia for old Europe—mountains, chalets, lakes, country estates. Even where people of color predominate, apparitions of whiteness inform the surroundings. The suburbs are pregnant with biblical fantasies of milk and honey.

Thus we have imaginary hills, viewless vistas, recumbent crests, concrete shorelines, and private commons, each simulation duplicating the empty reverie of colonization.

■ ■ ■

Children's growth serves as a universal measure of time. It meant little to me when I was ten or eleven and a strange adult would exclaim "back then you were only this tall," holding a palm a few feet from the floor. Now I'm that strange adult, telling befuddled children that they were just babies the last time I saw them.

Becoming another lame grown-up can be disconcerting, as can measuring age through memory. It's easy, and inevitable, to recognize our own evolution through the visible growth of other creatures. For me, the recognition evokes a sensual acknowledgment of mortality.

The youngsters on my bus will remain frozen as buoyant faces peering at me in the mirror, their smiles framed by missing teeth and ruddy cheeks. Perhaps I will see them again someday, but it's unlikely—and doubtful we'd even recognize one another after a significant passage of time. I gave them all my attention. I offered myself to loving ridicule. I lied in order to entertain. In turn, they provided me with a tremendous gift: a much-needed sense of purpose. I will miss them.

This job, which has never ceased to feel unexpected, provides a vista of things we're supposed to take for granted. Despite its stresses—early mornings, surprise inspections, tedious meetings, long hours—I needed the structure of routine and purpose, for as I would later learn (despite somehow already knowing), our built environment doesn't provide the peace it promises, only simulacra of peaceful living.

Still, I can't stop feeling like a fuckup, like a stargazer who made a mess of tidy destinies. The anxiety can be overwhelming, sometimes immobilizing. It grinds my abdomen and creates illusions of floating, of disembodied journeys through nebulous scenery. It is, in so many situations, an unsafe condition. For too many people around the world, anxiety is an intuitive reckoning with the imminence, and therefore the permanence, of dispossession.

Hateful expressions of love become a valuable currency on this kind of planet. Humans require better than enclosure in ugly, restrictive developments. Nobody can convince me that we're wired to enjoy counterfeit icons of leisure-class comfort. And so I struggle to find escape routes throughout each day, memorizing thoroughfares, tracking cul-de-sacs, because like all traitors to common wisdom, I refuse to abide motion without intersections.

The settlement with Illinois came out to over $800,000. A nice amount, for sure, but reduced almost to a third by lawyers' commissions and taxes. We paid off some debts and made some donations and then let the money sit in an account until we returned to the United States from Beirut. Once back, we used the remainder of the settlement to buy a townhouse in Northern Virginia, near family. The idea was that without a mortgage, we would be able to get by on one income (Diana's). It didn't end up being a great calculation. Between HOA dues and the million other expenses inside the United States, our remaining funds whittled away while Diana searched for a decent gig. Despite the decided advantage of owning a home, our position felt incredibly precarious. So I began looking around for job opportunities. Every time I passed an ad for bus drivers, ubiquitous in the schoolyards of Fairfax County, I paused to consider how cool it would be to drive one of those big yellow motherfuckers.

The settlement with Illinois came out to over $800,000. A nice amount for sure, but reduced almost to a third by lawyers' commissions and taxes. We paid off some debts and made some donations and then let the money sit in an account until we returned to the United States from Belize. Once back, we used the remainder of the settlement to buy a townhouse in Northern Virginia, near family. The idea was that without a mortgage, we would be able to survive on one income (Diana's). It didn't end up being a great calculation. Between HOA dues and the million other expenses inside the United States, our remaining funds withered away while Diana searched for a decent gig. Despite the decided advantage of owning a home, our position felt inherently precarious. So I began looking around for job opportunities. Every time I passed an ad for bus drivers – ubiquitous in the schoolyards of Fairfax County – I paused to consider how cool it would be to drive one of those big yellow motherfuckers.

The Influence of Anxiety

It began in 2007. I had been in Jordan with my father; our spouses remained stateside. He got on fine, with dozens of doting nieces and nephews keeping him flush with arak, but I decided to cut the trip short. Booze was never my thing.

I missed Diana and our small condo in Blacksburg, Virginia, but mostly I'd seen enough of Madaba, my father's hometown, despite the charm of its stone alleys and shabby storefronts, ambiance for a carnivalesque sense of tenor and motion. It was the time of year when many residents spent the night on verandas and rooftops.

We were staying in my uncle's flat, a spartan but comfortable space with two sitting rooms, built atop spice and jewelry shops. It used to be near the edge of town, but from my uncle's balcony, I could see an old agricultural valley, down past the portrait of Abdullah and Rania, rising into blocks of new construction.

Nothing was unusual. I'd been to Madaba many times and knew to expect a mixture of overbearing curiosity and easygoing chaos. I wanted out, though. I couldn't point to a particular urge, just a nagging desire to escape some unspecified dissatisfaction. Everything felt connected to a series of mishaps that had shepherded me to the Middle East in the first place. I took a bus to downtown Amman and argued my way into an earlier return ticket.

Two days later, I was at the old Alia airport, a bona fide dump, leaning against an escalator rail while waving to my dad standing in the departures lobby. He was taken aback when I told him I'd be

71

leaving but solicited no guilt or contrition. I suppose he chalked it up to the softness of early marriage. Perhaps he even granted me latitude by remembering when he was younger and more susceptible to emotion, inhabiting a world in which it would be unbearable to leave my mother.

In Madrid's coldly modern international terminal, I sprang for Wi-Fi and rented a one-way car from Dulles to Blacksburg. Anticipating fatigue on the drive, I found an electronics store and paid exorbitant prices for Guns N' Roses and Michael Jackson. I had quit smoking a year earlier (only to take it up again a few years later) and needed something to keep me engaged. Eurobeat and rural FM radio wouldn't do it.

I abused the rental car's little engine and finished the drive in three hours. Diana was waiting for me with lasagna, one of my favorite dishes. We ate with a sense of joy. Then I spent most of the night in the bathroom.

Getting sick had plenty of logical explanations. Eight hours on an airborne petri dish. Going from an empty stomach to 2,000 calories of dairy and carbs. An immune system compromised by fatigue. And God knows what festered in my intestinal tract after weeks of unrefrigerated street food. The illness lasted through the following night.

Then it returned after my next hearty meal. I quit eating heartily, opting for starchy fare, spiced with cayenne powder. The queasiness became less regular, but so did my food intake. Every few days I'd suffer nausea followed by nervous dietary restriction. My shirts started to sag around the neck and shoulders. I spent hours on the internet trying to find a diagnosis. Medical tests ruled out every condition that approximated my symptoms. A nurse suggested that I could be suffering anxiety. I found the notion ludicrous.

I continued the pathetic eating pattern, finding it difficult to leave the house in case I needed a bathroom. At a picnic in a public park, I was chatting with a colleague when suddenly I felt dizzy, a wave of static overwhelming my vision, sweat gathering on my forehead and scalp. I crumpled onto the grass. The colleague seemed less mortified than annoyed as Diana guided me to our car.

A few weeks later we attended a wedding in Madison, Wisconsin, where we had lived after grad school. As soon as we arrived, we went to Ian's, a by-the-slice pizza shop with playful toppings that had provided a weekly treat for three years. On the drive to the hotel, odd sensations accompanied the familiar nausea. It felt as if somebody had fired a glitter gun inside my extremities. I spent a sleepless night curled around four balled-up pillows. Things didn't improve in the morning. I managed to walk five blocks before stretching across a bench in the lobby of Monona Terrace.

Teaching required conversation and composure; I was generally up to the task. I arrived in the classroom feeling morbid, but left calm and content, sometimes lasting until dinner. Extracurriculars were out of the question, though. Writing, a reliable form of stress relief, was beyond my capability, and usually my desire. By late autumn, my diet consisted of Ensure and rice cakes.

We still managed to go out, which was bittersweet. I enjoyed the movement but longed for the normalcy that everyone else seemed to enjoy. During one excursion, we passed a store with a glass façade. My reflection revealed the gaunt remains of a once-operational human. It was clear that I would die if I didn't learn how to eat again.

■ ■ ■

Here I'm supposed to pivot into a contemplative tone and offer insight into mental illness, or perhaps recount the individual triumph that returned me to life. I can't follow convention, though, because I have no special knowledge and I still commune with specters of deprivation.

Recovering from anxiety is never an individual pursuit. I'm not sure recovery is even possible. Ultimately, the condition derives energy from structural forces and requires a communal solution. We can aim to manage physical manifestations of anxiety, but in the end it's a social disease.

My redemption story is straightforward: after weeks of resistance, I gave therapy a try. I came to love the therapist but refused medication. She convinced me otherwise, after minimal physical improvement. I tried some psychotropics. They freaked me out, but one of them restored my appetite. After stopping at a barbecue joint on a trip to North Carolina, I waited for nausea to ruin the drive, but my stomach contentedly digested almost a pound of potatoes and hush puppies. I still consider the aftermath of that meal a milestone.

Over the next few months, I gradually incorporated more foods into my diet, including pizza, my go-to comfort food. I'd be nervous for around two hours after eating, absorbing myself in all kinds of online silliness (much harder in the early days of social media). With the first flash of hunger, I could call it safe.

We visited Mexico to celebrate. Some habanero salad dressing actually made from pureed peppers (rather than being the pepper-flavored concoction of my gringo imagination) provided the only problem that I had with the food. I felt remarkably fortunate even as the sun stung my scalded lips for two days.

I knew things were better when an old pair of jeans, thirty-four inches at the waist, started feeling snug around my backside. I would soon outgrow them, shooting up four sizes in the next two years (hefty, but not quite Zizekian). As I write, struggling to excavate a truly bizarre episode, I am overweight (according to medical pundits, anyway), introverted but not agoraphobic, and consume plenty of food without fretting about nausea.

There are moments, though. Panic attacks arrive infrequently but abruptly. They've happened while I was giving a speech or out to dinner with acquaintances. The anxiety also assumes different manifestations. After an especially stressful day at work, I had trouble inhaling for two weeks. I'm apt to lightheadedness and a sense of detachment from physical surroundings. Worst of all, my body occasionally mimics the symptoms of a heart attack, with sharp chest pain and tingling in my fingers and toes.

You can call what I've described an eating disorder, depression, anguish, chemical imbalance, post-traumatic stress, introversion, whatever, but I'm partial to anxiety because it accommodates multiple connotations: excitement, nervousness, fear, worry, tension, foreboding, anticipation. I don't know any word, really, that properly describes what it means for the mind to express displeasure by devouring the body.

The term has settled into routine now that I consider myself functional. I've long been scared to sort through my experience of anxiety because I'm neither a physician nor a psychoanalyst. At its rawest, writing is a kind of testimony. So I approach you neither as a theorist nor an entertainer, but as a confessor submitting insecurity to the judgment of strangers.

■ ■ ■

Growing up in Southern Appalachia, we had a cranky neighbor, one of those "get off my lawn" types. (He literally screamed "get off my lawn" whenever we approached the property line.) He was a source of both terror and amusement. We provoked him but also took off whenever he approached, cane in hand.

I wanted to know what could inspire this kind of acrimony, so I asked my mom.

"Some people forget what it's like to be young," she explained.

■ ■ ■

Speaking only from my experience, panic attacks feel literally like death—or perhaps they hypostatize feelings of death from the unconscious. Those feelings are deeply subjective, so I can only try to describe their effects.

At the onset of a panic attack (or elevated anxiety or whatever you want to call it), not only do I feel as if I might die, but the sensation of death is palpable, even tactile, and almost calming in its air of inevitability. Doom washes over my intellection and a thought arises, clearly and rationally, "This is the end." I don't think about my son or wife or comforting moments from childhood. I should, according to popular accounts of near-death experiences, but that's not how it works for me. I think about how, come oblivion or recovery, the pain will soon end.

I imagine these attacks to be exactly what I'll feel in the moments before I actually die, which makes death less daunting. I now identify the outcome as a type of relief.

■ ■ ■

I hide in a corner of the dressing room, where dankness from pubescent armpits and faulty drainage likes to gather. I can hear their voices bouncing around the lockers one row over. Their faces have been close enough today. I no longer want to feel their breath near my earlobes. I no longer want to hear the language it carries. It's been a lifetime experience, this violent delegation into otherness.

We file onto the basketball court for aerobics (last week's lesson was square dancing; next week's will be wrestling). I've managed to escape their notice by lingering at the back of the group. Cachet, I understand at this point of my life, is impossible without humiliation. I am not reputable. I am the foreign object who provides raw material for the conqueror's social capital. So, I slink and skulk my way through a mandatory education designed far beyond our schoolhouse walls.

I trip over the workout step, letting out a yelp and eliciting a few stares. I'm still largely unnoticed, though. But it can't last. I'll soon be indexed by the teacher, the spectators, the building itself. I am too dark amid this uniformity, too indispensable in my expendability. Ever ignored, civilization will still insist on seeing me.

■ ■ ■

The frustrating thing about anxiety is its interplay with politics. The condition condemns its victims to relitigating ugly histories in unexpected places. Anxiety tends to emerge when compassion is restricted by popular notions of common sense.

Anxiety doesn't simply interact with politics; it conditions politics, as well. Social media discourses, for example, are replete with obvious expressions of anxiety. I recognize the patterns in my own commentary. Some people I just dislike. Immediately. It's not unusual. I imagine nearly all users have the same experience. We like to attribute dislike to taste or ideology, but it's worth considering whether taste and ideology quantify, rather than produce, the initial reaction. In many conflicts, I suspect, antagonism precedes disagreement.

In online interchanges, we don't always encounter rhetors, but exemplars of trauma. Even where they're not explicitly toxic, social media platforms can't satisfy our emotional needs. By pretending to have this ability, they make sure that bereavement will be the result of consumption.

A lot of conditioning establishes what we imagine to be visceral. Strong reaction to a face or a personality or a set of words is a form of self-defense. It needn't be logical or systematic. Anxiety is the emotional detritus of deliberate forgetting. People processing trauma want badly to remake the world. We get angry when potential friends appear to betray that desire.

My mother's insight has been a constant blessing in my life, but her theory about our angry neighbor was misplaced. Humans don't forget what it's like to be young. We remember it too damn well.

■ ■ ■

I'm not a brawler on social media. I'd like to say that I avoid conflict, but merely commenting invites confrontation. No matter how much restraint I attempt, I too squabble and remonstrate. Negative interactions can nag at me for hours, or days, beyond the strictures of logic. My stomach tightens and I have no appetite. I understand that I tricked myself into pursuing an outcome that cannot be granted.

The logic doesn't take, but I lean into it, anyway. What was the reason for my comment? For commenting at all? What point was I trying to prove? To whom? Was it the result of some deep-seated need to be correct? To be *recognized* as correct? Am I tacitly aware that political commentary isn't materialist, but material for the politics of online hierarchy? Have I reduced my sense of self to electronic branding? To validation through emoji? Is my participation an effort to escape the physical world? Or an attempt to negotiate its disturbances? Because you know those motherfuckers are always on the horizon, right?

People can point to a legitimate sense of community in certain sectors of social media, but they're fragile spaces, subject to quick accusations of apostasy or treason. In me, those spaces engender timidity and regret. I'll post something and then wonder what the hell I'm doing. People respond, but I'd breached a topic I don't care about enough to defend. Then I realize that I'm in no mood for hostility. I fret over wording, or being misunderstood, subject to a mobbing. I delete. I've no desire to entertain anxiety. These days it announces its approach.

Similar patterns exist offline, of course, but social media can offer platforms where people congregate to extract validation from strangers. Those platforms are perfect for conveying anxiety. They offer an important service to the ruling class, too. Social media taps into the same frustrations that compel people to riot.

Offline, anxiety is self-perpetuating, thanks to political culture and civil etiquette. Social life under capitalism necessitates repetition of trauma. The US system we're supposed to uplift has produced exceptional suffering. We're told that it's both possible and necessary to compartmentalize the past from the present, but these fantasies of linear progress only highlight the agonies of continued injustice. Theories of insurgency and upheaval can be deeply appealing; appeals to preserve a ravenous polity feel like a form of violence.

As for etiquette, I don't know how to explain it without sounding like the goal is to exonerate myself of rudeness—and it occurs to me that exonerating myself of rudeness may in fact be the point—but social and professional conventions disdain immobilization, which only compounds anxiety. The industrialized world isn't structured to benefit the demure or hesitant; civilized societies mistreat people that they deem unproductive. Avoidance is a terrific way to earn scorn.

It causes me tons of distress. My brain deadens in the face of simple tasks, like answering an email or a direct message. Even when I like the person who has solicited a response, even when I want to maintain a relationship, I can only stare at the screen, hopeless and angry, willing myself to answer. Come on, man! Something perfunctory. Start with a salutation. Then a sentence or two. That's it. I stare through hollow sockets before navigating away in shame.

Shame arises in similar fashion those thousands of times I let the phone ring, unwilling to honor whoever summons, or when I'm committed to a social function, even an apparently fun one, and can't drag myself anywhere near the door. It's a bizarre—what does one call it? affliction? sensibility? condition? illness? attitude? habituation?

I don't want to alienate friends and colleagues. I don't want them to dislike me or, worse, imagine that I dislike them. I want them to understand that I'm trying, but sometimes find myself locked into inexplicable paralysis. And yet I can't expect them to accept my absences. Who but a fellow misanthrope likes being ignored?

Social functionality and personal inhibition can be painfully discordant. Nobody's trained in the etiquette of reclusion. We judge the availability of others according to ego, attraction, status, and desire; mental illness is usually absent from the calculation.

■ ■ ■

As an undergrad I used to hang out in my favorite professor's office. A heavy smoker, she allowed me to light up as I pleased. (This shows that I'm old, yeah, but it was after the university had banned indoor smoking; the professor just didn't give a damn.) Her name was Rita Riddle, from Coeburn, Virginia, a tiny coal mining town near the Kentucky border. Her license plate read "Dr Mama."

She was a tough character, both unpopular and beloved. That sort of paradox defined her; she also alternated between brusqueness and candor. It depended on what mood her audience inspired. I learned to write under her guidance. She kept me in pocket money by assigning odd jobs around her house and yard. Mostly we chatted about epic works of film and literature: *The Godfather*, *Richard III*, *Mansfield Park*, *Citizen Kane*, *Moby Dick*. I've never met anybody with a better understanding of hubris and power.

"Dammit, boy, don't you ever become cynical," she'd demand. "Promise me." So I promised. We had the conversation a dozen times. It was important to Rita Riddle that I not become cynical. At the age of twenty, beholden to an unfamiliar future, it was an easy pledge. Youthful confidence is mainly a byproduct of ignorance, eroded in time by the strictures of civility, the stresses of family life, the silliness of politics, and the stupidity of education. Time and again I wanted to fail my mentor, something that would have been easy, a natural consequence of anguish, but I've not become cynical enough to break a promise.

■ ■ ■

During therapy, I discovered that my arrival from Jordan wasn't actually the beginning. I remembered that when a girlfriend dumped me in grad school, I suffered nausea every night for two months, sleeping with the bedroom and bathroom doors open so I could get to the toilet more easily. And I remembered the chest pains that I complained about in elementary school. My mom took me to specialists in Durham and Miami (where my grandmother lived at the time); I still harbor images of the electrode patches on my skeletal chest.

At the start of first grade, I cried until the school finally called my parents to cart me home. The memory is hazy, but I can put together a setting. Glistening floors. Antiseptic odors. Tiled walls. Dark stairs. Frustrated adults not bothering to whisper. A crushing, cavernous loneliness.

I loved kindergarten. The classrooms were four trailers in an old parking lot. They were relaxed and colorful. Children pounded the asphalt like jackhammers during recess. We napped side by side on foam cots. I learned to write love letters, to tie shoelaces, to grow flowers.

The main school was set back from the trailers, atop a steep hillside. The building still stands, still looks like a Victorian prison with its harsh angles and concrete inlays, a monument to scholastic austerity. There I was to be socialized, tempered, domesticated, shaped into a good boy anxious to learn the ways of the world. But I knew. I fucking knew. I didn't want to be near that goddamn building. Even at the age of five, I understood that death feels like the hypostasis of progress.

I had grown bitter—and, worse, conscious of my bitterness. I was proud of my decision to renounce academe and the pundit economy, but I still participated in those spaces as a spectator, an enormous mistake of both intellect and affection. Pride and happiness don't often intersect. Diana found a decent gig, at the University of the District of Columbia, and I was driving buses for the county. We had health insurance and food in the pantry. In many ways, we embodied the middle-class ideal supposedly under threat of extinction in the United States. There was nothing really to complain about, apart from the fact that we were living a middle-class ideal regrettably still in existence.

The Big Picture

When I was learning to be a school bus driver, our instructors talked often of the big picture. It was especially common during on-the-road training. An instructor would lean across the aisle and point to the windshield. "Remember the big picture." Something abnormal or noteworthy was ahead.

The big picture was meant to sharpen perception of roadway unpredictability: low-hanging branches, potholes, lane mergers, road construction, accidents, broken stoplights, standing water, fallen wires, erratic drivers. We were being trained to avoid problems through early detection.

I took to dispensing the line to unfortunate souls in my vicinity. "Think of the big picture," I'd intone knowingly whenever something didn't go according to plan. It wasn't always as annoying as it sounds. After I discovered a lump while showering, the big picture became a silly source of relief. Diana would complain about her workday.

"Remember my huevos, though," came the response. "Big picture."

When I complained, she'd say, "At least you have both of your balls. Big picture."

Although doctors declared the lump benign, it lives on as an uncouth metaphor for life's more pressing matters.

Then I got an idea. "The big picture" would make a tremendous self-help book. I could title it something like *The Big Picture: Life Lessons from Dr. School Bus Driver*. It would be the kind of shlock that corporate media like to promote and that rubes would buy by the boxful. Potholes are a metaphor for relationship troubles, before finding the perfect mate. Tree branches are unexpected career obstructions on the way to spectacular prosperity. Lane mergers signify familial closeness or new beginnings. Erratic drivers are haters trying to disrupt self-fulfillment. Standing water means a calm, collected soul. Shit, I could squeeze two or three books out of all the detritus on Northern Virginia's roadways.

Diana suggested turning the metaphor into a kid's book, an even better idea. A successful children's series is a gold mine. For years, I helped pay the mortgage on Mo Willems's brownstone. *Billy the School Bus* (or some such) goes on silly daily adventures, teaching the youth unexpected lessons. My inability to draw would be part of the charm.

In the end, I just can't do it. I'm too attached to the idea of writing as an avocation rather than a source of wealth. Maximizing earning potential by debasing an art so obliging of catharsis seems, I don't know, sacrilegious? Cynical? Ungrateful? The point of good writing is to illuminate, not exploit, anguish and vulnerability. I can't even bring myself to use Patreon. And so I proceed as usual in contented stupidity.

The metaphor can still be useful, though. The big picture. Potholes signify the physical damage from oppression. Tree branches are, let's say, the security state, always growing and encroaching on public space. Erratic drivers can represent any number of things: dippy politicians, social climbers, aunts and uncles, cocky kleptocrats.

And the standing water? That's easy. Standing water is the near future of low-lying land on this rotting planet.

■ ■ ■

In August, I began my second year as a school bus driver. Getting back into the seat after a nine-week break tested the limits of my fortitude. I was shocked by my resistance to the new school term. Summer break was shorter than what I enjoyed as a professor, but more relaxing—no nattering errands to worry about, no residual pettiness cluttering the inbox. Giving up an enjoyable routine was only part of the reason I dreaded getting back to work. The main reason was because two weeks before reporting, I visited South Africa.

I'm still lukewarm to public life, but when members of the academic freedom committee at the University of Cape Town invited me to deliver the 2019 TB Davie Memorial Lecture, I couldn't shelve my curiosity. After sitting on the invitation for a rude amount of time, I finally accepted. South Africa's inverted academic calendar eliminated work as an excuse to decline. I would have to overcome my timidity.

These days, moving through the sprawling tillage of modernity, I fluctuate between detached contentedness and immobilization generated by moments of tremendous sadness. South Africa fucked up the equilibrium. Less than an hour in Cape Town, a geological miracle, and my brain was transforming bad memories into wistfulness.

Table Mountain is the avatar of a million marketing efforts, but no photo does it justice. In person, it transcends portraiture, an ascending façade of sand- and mudstone, topped (during my visit) with plush, opaque rain clouds providing relief from a multiyear drought. Those clouds periodically tumbled down the cliff face, dousing the city with showers before dissipating to reveal the foggy plateau. The ocean is visible in almost every view, a reminder that we're at the tip of an enormous continent. All in all, it makes for a pleasant winter.

Cape Town isn't compact. The metropolitan area covers empty spaces between townships, suburbs, and urban sprawl. The architecture of colonization, Apartheid, racism, neoliberalism, and resistance is conspicuous in the mixture of abodes, reliable emblems of economic class: Dutch colonial estates, Tudor bungalows, glass skyscrapers, tin shacks, stucco duplexes, modern condos, shipping containers. The structures are enveloped by a stunning array of flora: candlewood, date palms, beech, stinkwood, turkey berry, willow, red pear, and Cape Saffron, a squat but lush specimen with deep green leaves and a rust-colored trunk.

On the way to the hotel, I remembered how pleasant it can be to travel, how we can reproduce a sense of belonging through provisional displacement. I was fascinated by Cape Town before arriving on the continent, starting at the boarding gate in Istanbul, where I saw a large crowd of people who weren't Black. A day later, I was trying to make sense of social relations too complicated for my range of comprehension. I couldn't locate a stable understanding of the place. I was a tourist fighting a backlog of simulacra, images of land and peoplehood extracted to the North and transmitted to the living rooms, bookshelves, and movie theaters of audiences eager to validate the superiority of their vanilla lives—verisimilitude as a profit scheme standing in for authenticity. It felt impossible to distinguish between visual immediacy and novelties of the colonial imagination. In turn, I contemplated my own disaggregation. Africa once again became the setting for a Westerner's psychological reckoning.

With a few hours to spare before obligations, I napped and showered, then popped half an Ativan before heading to the lobby, trying (and failing) to recall the etiquette of doctoral-level small talk. While waiting for my hosts to arrive, I stared through a picture window at the hotel garden, its shrubbery and flower beds streaked with rain, mesmerized by these forms of life that insist on growing amid tons of invisible poison. I could have left at that moment and been happy with the trip.

My hosts arrived and greeted me warmly. I was nervous, jumpy, but eased into the conversation. A few hours later, I was satisfied, animated, pleasantly infuriated all over again by the machinations of campus Zionists and their managerial allies. I liked the company, people who had much to teach me about South Africa and the world more broadly, fast-track friends versed in the magic of Southern hospitality. I stared at the outline of Table Mountain from my balcony late that night, trying to process a terrible realization: I had thoroughly enjoyed the evening.

The pleasure didn't abate. The following day, I seized the microphone without hesitation, reading from text I'd composed over months in piecemeal clauses at four in the morning. I slept heavily after the festivities. But in the background was the job I had left behind, and would soon resume, a reminder that the outing was only a temporary revival of an exanimate past. I began to resent the job, suddenly a tether to unadorned reality, reminding me that no transatlantic fantasy could erase the circumstances that made me worth inviting in the first place.

I returned to Virginia having forfeited the illusions of freedom that I worked so hard to create.

I spent the next few days in a state of dread. The parking lot; the streets; the stoplights; the subdivisions; the school bus itself—all were abstractions, no longer emblems of a halting catharsis, but reflections of a trauma I had voluntarily solicited. Cape Town: first my respite, now a geography of torment. It's bad news when fantasy is a form of stress.

In-service for work arrived, something of a day school for bus drivers. Five hours of information sessions. Then we selected our routes for the coming year. I'd earned enough seniority to not be the last to choose. After route selection: dry runs. This is when most of us get on the buses for the first time in two months and figure out where we'll be going on the first day of school. I approached my bus as an old friend with whom I no longer cared to socialize. It's a clunker, dinged and faded, with torn seats and a spiderweb crack on the front window, riding a chassis that clinks and clunks at any appreciable change of speed, but it's a blessedly reliable machine that I know more intimately than any other inanimate object.

The bus had an antiseptic smell, processed lemon and ammonium hydroxide, mixed with the balm of stagnant humidity. I botched the pre-trip inspection, having little recollection of the process that I had once studied so hard to memorize. I tucked my left-rights under a dashboard knob, guessing where they might be wrong, and slowly pulled into traffic. The bus was still hot after a few moments. Air conditioner: busted. Heat level: global warming.

I pulled onto a highway ramp, sweat dotting my bald head like bubble wrap, and gunned the engine, turning sharply to catch a breeze from the driver's window. Wind rushed into the compartment. Sheets of paper flapped into the stairwell. I barreled toward the flow of cars and grinned at the wonks I had bullied into the center lane. I was back in the seat. It felt fucking terrific.

■ ■ ■

When I was six or seven, my mom, figuring my bookishness might translate into something useful, bought me a microscope. It was a pale pastel blue with eggshell finish and a weighted base, a beautifully cheap piece of equipment. I immediately got to work.

"I want to look at a penny."

"A . . . penny?" She shook her head and left the room. (In retrospect, she was probably looking for the receipt.)

She returned, penny in hand. I clipped it under the screen and selected the biggest lens. Peering through the eyepiece, I saw only darkness. After tinkering with some knobs and switching lenses, I got the same result.

I had imagined something grander, a glistening copper plane stretching past the limit of my vision, the dips and ridges of Lincoln's face a topographic map of honor and prosperity. Still nothing tangible appeared. I soon grew bored of the darkness and returned to paperbacks. I couldn't comprehend microbes or particles. The things I wanted to see weren't visible with technology. The next day, my mom offered to take me to the library. I never saw the microscope again.

■ ■ ■

Figuring out the two-way radio is one of the hardest parts of school bus driving. One catches on quickly, but we received virtually no training for it, so proficiency comes through inference and practice. (Fucking up a call, transmitted to hundreds of people, isn't fun.) Like every transportation industry, we use dozens of "signals" and numerical codes. The point is to minimize clutter. We also want to prevent students from understanding the transmissions, especially during an emergency.

I'm kind enough to provide translations. If I see a kid listening to the chatter, I'll explain what's happening.

"Ha! These guys are gossiping and don't realize they're on the main channel."

"Ooh, this one's juicy. Two buses hit each other."

"There was a fight at the middle school. Everybody's leaving late."

"They don't have enough drivers, and nobody wants to volunteer."

"Accident on the beltway. All four lanes are closed. Ouch."

"Somebody's causing trouble on her bus and she wants the police to come."

"This dude doesn't know how to use the radio. The dispatcher is about to yell at him."

We can receive private calls, too. A private call is never good: it means a random drug test, time sheet problems, reminder of a meeting, surprise bus inspection, a request ("request") to cover another run, a summons to the main office, or some other thing that doesn't involve being left alone.

The radio is a specialized lexicon for the supposedly unskilled. It exists to efficiently disburse information, but most of it is noisy interference subjecting us to public judgment. It otherwise functions to collectivize individual anxiety. I diffuse the stress of hearing about everybody's problems by reverting to previous habits. Teachers teach, especially with a captive audience. It's impossible for me to not translate esoteric verbiage for the benefit of students who are meant to be excluded.

■ ■ ■

A couple of weeks into the school year and I was over the uncertainty of South Africa, although the experience illustrated that no amount of bitterness or cynicism will untether me from my original avocation. It's a strange sort of liminality, exile combined with disgust, which distorts my sense of belonging. The school bus or the campus? I can function in both spaces, but neither feels comprehensive or permanent; contradiction is the only steady variable.

I remind myself why I pursued this line of work. Movement. Contact. Anonymity. No political cliques. No hermetic architecture. No dress code.

Unpredictability was also an attraction. I knew it wouldn't be the kind of gig to bog down in stasis. Drivers deal with youngsters apt to moodiness and rebellion. A kindergartner can get a random nosebleed. The entire bus can erupt into a paper ball fight. Students can throw objects at passing cars. Sixth graders can catcall a woman sunbathing on her lawn. Riders up front can record the driver obliviously singing "Be My Baby." (All of these things actually happened, by the way.)

It's been a steep learning curve for somebody accustomed to college students. Middle schoolers are the biggest challenge. Many drivers have difficulty with elementary schoolchildren, but I'm good with that age group and know lots of tricks to manage their attention. The task requires serious energy, though. High schoolers tend to get lost in teenage drama and/or smartphones. Despite their reputation as hellions with ill-developed brains, I've found them to be polite and thoughtful.

But middle schoolers flummox me. Being my normal easygoing self is an invitation to chaos, impossible to curtail once unleashed. Playing the role of stern bossman hasn't worked, either. (It's an unnatural conceit for me, something I'm sure the students easily recognize.) After finding numerous globs of gum stuck to the bus floor, I decided to raise the issue before releasing them to school one morning. I stood at the front of the aisle and addressed them with what I imagined to be a glare and a snarl.

"Pay attention," I barked. "I've noticed gum stuck to the floor of this bus numerous times. Anyone care to guess how the county gets rid of gum on the floor?"

Most of the students tried to slouch out of view. "They make you clean it?" one of them finally ventured.

"Correct. I get down on my knees and scrape it up, which is as disgusting as it sounds. So I'm gonna make this simple for you," I finished, using a line I'd practiced in my head throughout the run, "If you insist on making this bus ride unpleasant for me, I promise that I'll make it unpleasant for you." I crossed my arms and narrowed my eyes as they filed off the bus.

After the PM run with the same students, I did my usual check of the bus. On the floorboard between the two back seats, like a glistening symbol of karmic putty, was a fresh wad of white chewing gum.

Beyond the appeal of unpredictability, I liked the idea of earning a living beyond an economy of self-absorption in spaces (academe, journalism, social media) where participants monetize a brand and sell banality to co-ideologues and cultural influencers. I don't want to see the world from the perspective of Westerners who travel to sites of conflict in the news (that is, places where the US ruling class is organizing its greed) and put their faces in the foreground of the action. They become avatars of the story, translating the misfortune of foreigners into self-indulgence, and thus serve as handmaids of the elite, no matter how adamantly they claim to inhabit virtuous cartographies. Information equals extraction. Content is currency. Value accrues in service to the content's producer. News is birthed from self-invention. What audiences come to understand as an event only exists because of the interloper's latent power. The entire production is a setup for narcissistic grotesquerie.

How to write in these conditions of exploitation? Where to travel for stories that don't bleed the locals? If I knew the answers, I'd happily share them. My compromise was to derive material from necessary motion, a new and novel livelihood, nearly absent as a setting in both fiction and nonfiction. I post essays to a basic WordPress design, without worrying over deadlines and editorial politics. I barely know how to operate the site: I can upload and edit entries and create a thumbnail picture; everything else is a mystery. I dislike paywalls and don't really care about page clicks. My goal is to create a decent body of writing in a space conducive to experimentation. That writing will be seen or ignored according to the wishes of its audience.

Driving frees me from the economic stresses of a putrid industry. Writing allows me to extract creative value from wage labor. It might be a stretch to say it's good, but liminality isn't altogether bad, either.

■ ■ ■

Last June, two days before the end of the school year, we had our final team meeting in a middle school's multipurpose room. The period was hectic. Schools let out at irregular times. Afternoons were filled with thunderstorms. Kids were amped up. We had to deep clean our buses and submit them to inspection.

The entire two-hour meeting consisted of a team-building exercise. I like my supervisors—they're bus drivers, too, and that's important—but a team-building exercise at the end of the year? I soon realized it was their first time curating that sort of effort.

The supervisors passed out balloons and asked each of us to take a Post-it note. We were to write down a question meant to illuminate something meaningful about a colleague and then stuff it into the balloon. The task required multiple explanations. "Questions?" everyone asked. We inflated our balloons with varying levels of success (easy to tell who was involved in their children's birthday parties). Some of my colleagues seemed confused, which in turn caused me confusion. It was obvious what we were getting ready to do. Academe had prepared me well for hot air.

We stood in a large circle, about seventy-five of us, and punched the balloons into the middle. A great mess of them descended onto the floor. Once we had grabbed a new balloon, the supervisors instructed us to burst it and retrieve the note, something most of us performed with glee. As my colleagues stomped on their catch, creating a barrage of popping sounds, I retreated into a corner. I didn't want to be exposed when a SWAT team kicked in the door.

I unfolded my slip of paper. "Why u do this job?"

I tried to think of a short, diplomatic answer as we returned to our seats. "All right, we'll start over here," one of the supervisors said, pointing across the room. A middle-aged woman squinted and read, "When do we select summer routes?"

The room filled with nods and murmurs. "We'll answer that later," the supervisor responded. "Who's next?"

The person to the woman's left held up his note. "Why ... not ... more ... overtime?" he sputtered. More nods and murmurs, louder this time.

"Okay, everyone," the supervisor interjected. "We're not looking for technical questions. We want things that can tell us about each other."

"But what about overtime?" somebody shouted from the back.

The supervisor ignored him and pointed to the next reader.

"Will we have raises next year?"

I felt bad for the supervisor as she struggled to repel a facepalm. "Listen, guys, I'll answer these questions at the end of the meeting for anybody interested." She tried her luck at a different table.

"In what city were you born?" an elderly man read in halting English. My question. I schemed ways to get credit for putting us on the right track.

"Um, yes," the man answered. "I was born near a place called Ho Chi Minh City. It used to be called Saigon. When we kicked out the Americans, it became Ho Chi Minh City. I'm from there." I was happy to be on this guy's team.

The exercise continued with a preponderance of technical questions. When it was time to answer, "Why u do this job?" I muttered something about choosing a field that seemed fun and unpredictable. I then stuffed the note into the back pocket of my jeans and daydreamed alongside my coworkers about all that had gone unanswered.

■ ■ ■

The little ones like to play show-and-tell while boarding the bus. They stop next to my seat and display new shoes, drawings, toys, trading cards, electronics—anything, really, that facilitates self-esteem. I respond with the proper ebullience. My self-esteem isn't isolated from theirs.

I never expected the shy, stuttering boy to upset convention. He's the picture of gawky, prepubescent childhood: grungy hair, patchwork teeth, gangly posture, spindly legs. "My-my-my father is waiting outside," he tells me every afternoon.

"Go say hi to him, then." The boy has no idea I'm being rude.

He stopped in front of me one morning with an unusual contraption. "An, um, a, m-microscope," he announced. It looked brittle, more toy than utensil, and yet it was lovely for the breadth of its simplicity.

"What do you want to look at?"

"B-b-bugs and stuff."

"Be careful with it, now. Don't let it get damaged on the bus."

He pressed the microscope against his chest and ambled toward his seat. I mentally walked alongside him, picturing the space from the perspective of its passengers, carried along to buildings that will be much larger in memory than their physical stature. The little boy had enlightened the middle-aged man. I wasn't completely foolish, nearly forty years ago, to imagine an item of small value as a grand object; I had merely stumbled into a conception of history that I wouldn't understand for another thirty-five years. An event isn't measured by size, but by gravity. Consider the enormity of diseased and emaciated babies, of dead Palestinian children in ice cream freezers, of teenagers conscripted into slavery for the pleasure of wealthy men, of centuries of civilization predicated on abuse and debasement: amplifying the particles of human life requires no scientific machinery.

■ ■ ■

It's rare that school bus drivers make the news, unless one has been negligent or unlucky, but a few weeks ago I read about a seventy-one-year-old driver in Minnesota who declined to greet his Central American passengers with a customary "good morning." A devotee of Donald Trump, the driver wouldn't confess to racist inclinations. He instead cited tradition, language, crime, demographics, and economic anxiety—all the things, in other words, that incline people to racism.

Although the story lacks the sensationalism of a multivehicle accident, exotic roadkill, or missing children, it gets at something fundamental to the peculiar culture of school transportation. It's not normal in most professions for a perfunctory greeting to symbolize competence. For school bus drivers, though, the banality of a mechanical "good morning" is deeply important.

The act conveys meaningful information to students: I acknowledge you; I care about your safety; I won't judge you by language or appearance; everyone deserves a platitude; you are welcome here. The act can subtly do more complex work, too. I don't want your day to be filled with unhappiness; I'd like to help put you in the right mood to learn; I too dread this journey to school; (try to enjoy it); I'll be waiting for you at the end of the day. That simple greeting, so often a formality, can be a critical lesson in the tacit power of everyday communication.

The greeting is different in the shadows of a street side than it is in the lobby of a commercial building because we're not carting children to random destinations, but to places entrusted with their welfare, capable of producing both happiness and trauma. And we're largely invisible. The conveyance, not the driver, attracts and occupies attention. The act of speaking, then, reassures the children that they aren't anonymous organisms in a mechanized apparatus.

Withholding formalities can be disorienting because we're attached to them as social conventions (nothing becomes conventional without a meaningful origin). The driver in Minnesota fails the children he's entrusted to safeguard because his silence excludes them from the dignity of a civic life. He communicates politics through that silence, one the children easily understand. They begin their school day anxious that they don't belong, that they're aliens and interlopers, unwanted, distrusted—feelings added to extant barriers of class and language. This stuff cultivates insecurity and self-doubt. There's your achievement gap, articulated in the silences of vulgar nostalgia.

The driver's version of that nostalgia is especially toxic. He's beholden to myths of progress and forward motion—he can't do his job without creating movement—and yet he's immobilized by visions of an archaic past, one that can be remembered as utopian only by people who enjoyed its malignancy. I don't feel sorry for him. The children he ignores deserve whatever empathy we're liable to offer. The driver is good for one thing: he reminds us that no matter the salary or status, nobody's job, in a world structured by inequality, is unimportant.

■ ■ ■

It used to take me four or five weeks to learn names in classes with small enrollments, so there was never much hope of learning names in a busful of rowdy children. The only logical option was to give them nicknames.

I began with myself.

When I started driving last year, younger elementary kids wanted to know my name. Fourth and fifth graders didn't seem to care. It was the same at the start of this school year. On the first day, they mostly rode in silence. They didn't know what type of person I am, volatile or laidback (I'm both, but I don't like expressing volatility), and they're preoccupied by traveling into new environments. When they're comfortable enough to ask questions, I provide silly answers, so they'll know it's okay to cut loose. One of the pleasures of my job is turning over a gaggle of maniacal children to their teachers.

So this year when they asked my name, I knew I would lie, but I was too worried about staying on course to have concocted a lie in advance. "Bus driver! What's your name?" I started thinking about things in the news before exclaiming, "My name is Mister Fried Chicken Sandwich."

Immediately they all wanted to be named after food items. "Guess my name! Guess my name!" The chorus reverberated throughout the bus's sticky interior.

"Let's see . . . you're Macaroni and Cheese."

"You're Vegetable Lasagna."

"And you're Supreme Pizza."

On it went until I ran out of dishes that I imagined would sound familiar. I realized the problem I'd created for myself the next morning when they asked me to repeat their names.

"That's not my name! I'm Spaghetti and Meatballs, remember?"

Sure, kid.

"Hey, you said I'm Mashed Potatoes!"

I did?

And yet I can't get high schoolers to interact with me. The other day I overheard a conversation tailor-made for my intervention.

"Is Harvard in Pennsylvania?" a boy asked.

"Pennsylvania?" another student laughed. "It's in Connecticut, dumbass."

"I can't tell if you're joking," I piped up, "but Yale is in Connecticut. Harvard is in Massachusetts." They sheepishly glanced in my direction and returned to their conversation. I wanted to add, "I've given talks at both places," but it wouldn't have commanded their interest. I'm mostly nonspecific to them, although almost to a person they thank me when exiting the bus. It's a decent arrangement. The environment mitigates any professional identity crisis I'm apt to experience and the students can discuss their futures without worrying about the kind of example I set.

Self-invention on a school bus isn't the glamorous stuff of elite academe or globetrotting punditry, but in its own humble context no less pronounced. For instance, I'd rather eat thumbtacks than a fried chicken sandwich.

• • •

Amid a hot, dry fall, the landscape in Virginia is disoriented—bare trees without the preceding foliage, an autumnal atmosphere subsumed to summertime haze—so driving is more difficult because of persistent mugginess and the fatigue it generates, but I think of the condition as just another surreal feature of a new life I still don't recognize ("am I really driving this big-ass school bus?") after spending years picturing a profuse future of ideas and accolades and interchange, a specious concept of accomplishment trying to pull me away from the safety of a glass and metal enclosure into an unreality I badly want to leave behind.

■ ■ ■

"Look, the kids on the bus in front of us are waving."

"I'm not waving back. I don't want to encourage them."

"They're still waving. It's bus number six."

"Did you know that their driver is named Teddy?"

"Nuh-uh. Do you call him Teddy Bear?"

"I'm not sure he'd like that. When I was a kid, my barber was named Teddy Bear . . . Seriously."

"Is he still your barber?"

"Do I look like I need a barber?"

■ ■ ■

It's been nearly a year since I started this job, nearly three years since I last taught a college course. I wish I had useful advice for people who experience midlife career transitions, but I'm still not sure what I've learned. There's a large body of work about leaving academe, known as "quit lit," and inconsistency is its most notable feature. Some people left because they were trapped in adjunct purgatory, others because job security made them miserable. Some were fired. Others were bullied out. It's a bitter genre.

Ambivalence is always evident in these pieces, because no matter how much the authors hated it, academe isn't easily expunged from the mind or body. Getting a doctorate requires a long gestation period predicated on persistent acculturation. Self-worth is coterminous with status. Much of the learning happens off the books—developing the indispensable skills of sycophancy and artful supposition.

But there's also something beautiful about working with students, trying to inhabit the world in abstractions and sharing epiphanies with like-minded people. The ideal of campus provides meaning and yet the same ideal so adeptly produces exasperation, self-loathing, and alienation. It's a heavy feeling to discover that the university is a corporate organ wherein the life of the mind is less a regime than an ad campaign. That realization produces a hard kind of disappointment, the disappointment of existing in a fallen world.

My transition into school bus driving has intensified the feeling. I'm more skeptical, but less misanthropic. I don't know how to integrate what I miss about academe with what I enjoy about no longer being an academic. I want to say that both spaces are fundamentally the same, but they're not. The world looks different when you're the source of extraction. My only advice to fellow ex-academics is to be resilient because a part of you will always yearn to revive the same fantasies you decisively rejected. Academe is a scar impervious to cosmetic surgery.

The influence of my past life conjures intense loneliness and a persistent sense of disbelief. I can't listen to credentialed voices any longer without envisioning opportunism and manipulation. It's both an overcompensation and a statement of class solidarity. The bitterness and negativity I supposedly exhibit, so distasteful to guardians of rhetorical etiquette, are byproducts of freedom. These days, saying that I want Zionist settlers to disappear is merely chitchat, the language of storefronts and cafés in hundreds of cities. I can use the word "Palestine" around my colleagues without internal dread or fear of retribution. It's people with microscopic vision who transform the mundane into a national emergency.

Take the "working class" of leftist punditry. It's a formation invented in classrooms and boutique periodicals. Those who inhabit the category don't want the luxuries that our well-bred champions promise. The promise, in fact, is an insult, a way to justify the pundits' upper-class predilections, for them to consume at our expense while maintaining credibility as *People of the people*. No worker that I know looks to these People for guidance, information, or analysis. It's only because I'm a lapsed academic that I even know they exist.

The working class that I inhabit is skeptical, heterodox, and international, in many ways a reflection of academe's self-image, without the comfort or pretension. My coworkers exhibit a rough-hewn understanding of what struggle means beyond the insipidness of affectation and sloganeering. Professional analyses of the demographic rarely comprehend or reproduce the sensibility. I'm sure that some of my coworkers have reactionary opinions, but they're largely tucked behind our interests as county employees hustling the necessary hours to survive in an expensive region. The troublemakers among us are also furtive, but not difficult to identify when they feel like talking. Even the most conservative bus driver behaves more radically in relation to management than the typical Marxist professor. Loyalty to the group is baked into the culture, evident the moment a newbie walks into the training center. Nobody needs to discourse about it.

■ ■ ■

I entered the hotel room. With a cream color scheme and baby blue trimmings, sleek appliances and brass fixtures, the space managed to look both contemporary and traditional. I turned on the bedside lamps and pulled my laptop from the desk drawer. It had been a long but satisfying evening. I wanted to relax on the balcony before lying in bed.

Fog lingered on the other side of the railing, draping the roof of a squat building across the courtyard, before elevating into a thick canopy over Table Mountain. The air smelled of damp wood and seawater. It was quiet in this part of the city. A car whooshed in the distance every few seconds and bursts of wind crackled through tree branches, but otherwise nightfall had asserted supremacy in this part of town. Only my frenetic energy disturbed the peaceful atmosphere.

I scrolled through the speech that I would give the next evening, steeling myself to revive a skillset that I had murdered. I didn't know if I could read anymore while making eye contact or go off script during question and answer. It had been a long time. I wanted to make good on the opportunity.

I remembered what one of the hosts, Elelwani Ramugondo, had advised before bidding me goodnight: "Say a prayer. You see, in the end you're not trying to reach people's minds, but their spirits." I didn't understand her meaning at first. On the balcony, engulfed in the luminescence of a foggy landscape, I realized that Elelwani had decoded the structure of my ambivalence. I loathe economies of talking, in which opining acts as an economic incentive, because their fundamental goal is to get the wrong people to listen. Our objective, so rich in South Africa's history, is to strengthen humanity from below as a continuous repudiation of injustice. Those in power will necessarily hate the effort.

It was late. Tomorrow would be busy. I went inside and undressed for bed. In the back, left pocket of my jeans, pressed against the room key, was a slip of folded yellow paper. I opened it and read, "Why u do this job?"

Dread engulfed me. In two weeks, I'd need to be back in the seat, but the prospect was inconceivable. I thought about the moment when I originally held the note, at the end of a seemingly interminable school year. How could I start again at the beginning? I balled up the jeans and tossed them beside the entertainment stand. Bus drivers aren't conditioned for luxury accommodations. Professors aren't accustomed to the maladies of physical labor. I needed sleep.

The task proved difficult. I played the question repeatedly in my foggy brain, struggling to see the big picture. The attempt created a lot of noise, until the final seconds of consciousness. I woke up a few hours later and stumbled onto the balcony with a cold cup of coffee and a pack of smokes. It's not really a job, I realized, gazing into the pitch-dark ether, cleared of its overcast by a chilly wind blowing down the cliff face. It's more of a spiritual occupation.

There are many ways to lose a job. Getting fired is the most obvious form of job loss, and certainly the most notable. But people also resign, move, emend, rebel, matriculate, disappear, or fall ill. Sometimes jobs are temporary. Sometimes jobs just go away.

The Anxiety of Insignificance

It's not hard to remember the week in which COVID-19 became a social monster. We had been hearing about a distant pandemic for a month or two, but it was off in China, a place Americans are trained to think of as unsanitary. By the first week of March, though, it was pretty clear that some kind of illness was coming. Even to the amazingly advanced and enlightened United States (which would prove uniquely ill-equipped to handle a public health crisis). The new virus had breached our heavily guarded frontiers and would soon overwhelm the entire country.

I vividly recall what seem like random things about that week (but things that at the time felt important): Tom Hanks and Rita Wilson caught COVID; the NCAA college basketball tournament was shut down; NBA player Rudy Gobert joked around by touching and coughing on a bunch of microphones, just before testing positive along with much of his team (more people remember than Gobert likely prefers).

I also recall medical pundits gravely warning us that in a worst-case scenario we could be locked down for two weeks. I'm not *that* kind of doctor, but I knew the forecast was unsound. You have to be a spectacular mark to buy that kind of sunshine.

My nephew had a birthday party on March 7th at one of those trampoline places with lousy arcades and massage chairs that beep if you sit in them without inserting money. Beyond the usual stuff, it was a weird vibe. The pandemic was already ravaging Seattle and New

York City. China was fully locked down, as were Italy and Spain. You could feel something weird in the air. (Something you could name as viral particles if you cared to be specific.) Nobody was wearing a mask, but people were thinking about the pandemic. You could tell by their body language. Maybe we were talking about it. I don't recall. I kept going to the bathroom to wash my hands.

It would be the last public event I attended that year. The following week shattered any lingering illusions; we were dealing with a very real pandemic. (The arguments over COVID's danger and public health measures were instantaneous.) I couldn't stop regretting how much I had complained during the monster truck rally I went to in February. In retrospect, it was a wonderful time. Maybe I deserved to sit at home.

By that March, I had moved into a substitute bus driving role. Persistent anxiety was making it more difficult to concentrate, and Diana had found a job with good health insurance. As a substitute, I could choose from different shifts throughout the week and grab open routes close to home. It was a nice arrangement. I liked the challenge of covering different routes and was experienced enough that getting lost was no longer a foregone conclusion. (I don't think I got lost even once.)

But on that Friday of the second week of March—when sports tournaments were cancelled and celebrities were catching ill—it was clear that schools would be closing. I parked the bus after my PM shift and lingered before going to my car. It was unusually quiet. I was the last one in and nearly all the school employees had left. I locked the door and the various outside compartments and thought, "Yeah I won't be doing this again for a while."

I arrived home to the news that schools would be moving online, effective immediately. All transportation was grounded. The next day, my brother and a friend wanted to try a restaurant in DC. I chickened out.

I don't normally remember past events so clearly. But that week is still fresh in my mind. I knew that drivers were likely to be paid even without routes to cover. Still, it's not often that a sabbatical feels so dreadful.

■ ■ ■

A few months before making the switch from full to part time, I decided to write a novel. I wanted to continue driving but couldn't find a balance between a full-time job and my sudden literary aspirations. It was particularly difficult keeping pace with my thoughts while at work. There wasn't enough time to record ideas, not in outline and certainly not in narrative. Even when my bus was extremely loud, I was daydreaming ideas about plot and dialogue that would disappear by the time I got to my laptop.

After I decided to leave academe for good, I became a different kind of writer. My output was no longer tied to career incentives, and I could now bang away on the keyboard as a form of leisure or catharsis. Deadlines no longer mattered, so irregularity became a habit. Various pressures still existed—they always do, otherwise writing would be incurably dull—but it was nice to decommodify the practice. Quality of publisher suddenly mattered much less than quality of publication. In fact, a piece of writing didn't need to be published at all. My hard drive is filled with abandoned documents in various stages of completion.

I also felt less pressure to perform the usual service expectations of a professor—the stuff they do without direct remuneration, for the good of the field. Or maybe the pressure to serve was repurposed toward pleasing a different audience. Whatever the case, it was no longer important to complete a thousand unsatisfying errands. And I didn't have to remember which obscure website or podcast I gave an interview to. My CV happily moldered in obscurity.

People still asked me to peer review manuscripts or to provide blurbs and I usually tried to be helpful, at least up to the point that merely thinking about service to the industry made me ill. I wanted to be of use to former colleagues—the ones I respected, anyway—and play some kind of role in the life of the mind, or whatever true believers like to call it, but I couldn't shake the sense that I was volunteering myself for exploitation. I wasn't happy during that period while contributing to an academic project. It was labor without the benefit of employment. My reaction was sometimes petulant: the industry made clear that it didn't want my input, so why should I participate? The only thing motivating me was an archaic sense of obligation. I tried to separate personal relationships from professional duties but learned that it's not an easy task. For me it was damn near impossible. The industry has a way of insidiously disrupting organic feelings of camaraderie, of making us feel like we're forever trying to decode the terms and conditions of an implicit arrangement. Maybe that describes every interaction under capitalism. I wasn't motivated to work out the details. All I knew is that no bus driver had ever fucked me over.

No interaction is unsullied by self-interest (which can mean anything from breathing to behaving as a sociopath). Purity of intent or outcome is a fantasy. Uncertainty (and often distrust) mediates ideals of friendship. Thus we scour assorted strata of society to find subcultures where the economy of self-promotion isn't so great a burden that intimacy and gratitude become hopeless, or we retreat to the default of filial kinship, for better or worse. Academe happens to be one of the most difficult places to locate any of these things. Institutional forces expertly reduce normal human interplay into nonstop cultures of transaction.

And to be perfectly honest, participating in that grind isn't worthwhile without a paycheck and a package of benefits.

That's the thing apostates need to understand: if you leave, then leave properly. It's difficult to keep partially engaged, something like the equivalent of a nicotine addict deciding to have just one cigarette a week. Chances are you'll soon be sneaking into 7-Eleven to buy an entire carton.

■ ■ ■

It was easier to be a bus driver and a novelist than a bus driver and an occasional academic. The former is a more natural pairing. Novelists emerge from all kinds of professions. Professors emerge from graduate school, along with the occasional art-world luminary or war criminal.

Some jobs lend themselves to writing. Others leave little time for extracurriculars. School bus driving does both. It offers plenty of time to think and a sizable gap in the middle of the workday, but it also requires early mornings and the ability to be constantly alert (meaning early nights, as well). The few-hour break between morning and afternoon shifts isn't especially valuable for an aspiring novelist. Errands need running, dinner needs prepping, and naps need taking. And that's if you don't have to drive the vehicle to the garage or get stuck with a midday run.

Each day after work, I devoted time to my son—eating a leisurely dinner, playing Uno, kicking a soccer ball around the parking lot, or simply vegging on the couch to whichever Nickelodeon sitcom he was into that week. I was keen to make up for not being around in the morning, a time of bonding that I missed dearly, ever since my first day at the training center. In earlier days, I would do a bit of writing after my son went to bed, but anymore I would fall asleep shortly after.

I wouldn't abjure parental responsibilities, but I wanted to write. In my experience, fatherhood was largely incompatible with literary aspirations because I felt terrible guilt taking on an individualistic enterprise with a lonely child in the house. Even now, around two weeks after my son turned ten, I suffer remorse for so often surrendering to narcissistic urges. I'm sure there are hundreds of things I could have done better, and could do better in the present, but I've come to accept that I'll never separate feelings of shame from parenthood.

The best time for writing was early in the morning while the car warmed up. The parking lot was in back of our building, accessible through the lowest level of our townhouse. I'd trudge into the lot and start the engine, then give myself ten minutes to write in the dim basement light. Those little sessions could be productive. The output was always meager but of high quality. Whatever I wrote in those fast-moving minutes was informed by desperation, by a tremendous hunger to succeed in an unwelcoming industry. I didn't want to be an author. I wanted to be able to write for a living. Neither the near impossibility of that goal nor middle age could slow my ambition. When I read my novels, I can always tell which parts were written during those ten-minute interludes between waking up and driving to work. The language of those sections is incredibly energetic, almost fervent, and I wonder how I ever found that kind of enthusiasm.

Otherwise, I stole a moment or two at the computer during midday break or just before bed. On the weekends, I dodged unnecessary social obligations and tried to write in volume. The goal was 2,000 words per day. It rarely happened, and the pace left me with a lot of editing at the end of it all. But that didn't bother me. I had to make this new thing happen.

Then the pandemic came.

Hypothetically, it would have allowed more time to write. In reality, it simply changed the dynamics in such a way that routine became unthinkable. I got the mornings back with my son, but also became his caretaker amid the new frontier of remote learning. It was largely miserable.

My pathetic understanding of even basic technology made me a bad candidate to chaperone online schooling. It took my son less than a week to figure out how to navigate multiple tabs, with only one, if I was lucky, having anything to do with class. On his first day, I stomped around the living room asking, "are you *sure* that microphone is off?" every two minutes. He was sick of me before lunch.

I still don't know how to log onto his school dashboard and just have to believe him when he says he has no homework.

I'd like to blame computer illiteracy for my subpar performance as a stay-at-home dad, but other flaws quickly became apparent—namely a short fuse whenever my son slagged off his assignments. I'm what you might call a lenient parent, and the initial period of lockdown was the only time my son and I have ever fought. In second grade when the virus arrived, my son simply wasn't inclined to online learning. (I doubt if any second grader has that sort of inclination.) Up to that point, we had no problems: his teachers sent good reports, he didn't exhibit abnormal tendencies, and he loved going to school, something I outgrew the summer after kindergarten. In an online milieu, though, he was defiant and temperamental. I spoke with him calmly. I tried to reason. (The notion that children don't reason, or don't respond to reason, is stupid and self-defeating—most of the time.) I told stories of my frustrations as a student. I busted out my corniest jokes. He was having none of it. He assumed an air of grandiose indifference and spent all his creative energy on being delinquent. After a while, I would lose patience and raise my voice or wave my arms and he would storm away. It seems like a long time ago, now that we're back to the usual conviviality. Still, seeing that I had passed along my obstinance to an innocent child left me with a terrible self-loathing that will probably never go away. Eventually, we grew accustomed to the strange new situation, and I can only wonder (with horror) how many parents and children had it worse. Already the traumas of so much insecurity are evident in society at large. Not everyone is lucky enough to sublimate those traumas into works of artistic merit.

There was a constant gloominess in Northern Virginia at the beginning of the pandemic. The sky was usually cast in some kind of gray, with a cold wind blowing from the northwest. The physical environment informed the region's general mood. My family tried to get outside despite the bad weather. A gloomy outdoors is better than a cheerful interior. We quickly learned to ignore the film of moisture that collected on our hands and cheeks from the constant drizzle. I wondered at the time if I'd look back on those days fondly. Two years later I still don't have an answer. Any image involving a moment of togetherness with my wife and child provides a fond memory, but I also remember a relentless tension and uncertainty.

■ ■ ■

My son's eighth birthday passed and he didn't get to have a party. He spent the day watching TV and eating junk food. Although he seemed content, Diana and I were crushed. Like most seven-and-a-half-year-olds, he had spoken excitedly about the kind of party that he wanted. None of his ideas involved social distancing.

(This is one reason why I disliked the argument that we shouldn't complain about, or mourn, the loss of little rituals because not dying is enough. Living isn't the same as being alive. And many of the rituals wiped out by social distancing are critical to a meaningful existence.)

Easter season was upon us and there would be no large family gatherings, a huge feature of my son's life up to that point. I didn't mind being isolated, but worried about its impact on him. Chaotic get-togethers are a mainstay of our cultural identity.

A few days after his birthday, a package arrived on our front porch. It was long and only a couple of inches thick. His uncle had bought him a skateboard—and not a toy version either. My son went wild, of course, but I figured that after a day or two of frustration he'd lose interest. That was his pattern: get into something, do it for a while, give up. He'd been asking about a skateboard since he was a toddler, but I never took it seriously. He also wanted to be Spiderman.

The first day was rough. He couldn't get onto the thing without falling. I wasn't any help. Every time I tried to demonstrate, I ended up on my ass. Forward progress was even harder. I ran beside him as he moved along at a speed more advanced than middle age, both of his hands grasping my outstretched forearm. He allowed me to pant for a few moments before we took off in the opposite direction. Another week, tops, I predicted.

But on the second day, he let go of my forearm. For a second or two at first, and then for long distances as I trotted alongside him. Soon he was going down small inclines and then full-blown hills. He raced ahead of me and I stood back in disbelief. That was my baby zipping in and out of parking lots. He looked like a little adult. By day three, he could kick-push-and-coast down the entire block. On day four, he was doing U-turns.

A week later, he was learning to stop and to control the angle of the board with his back foot. With me lifting him by the armpits, he was also trying out simple tricks. It takes a long time to master any of this stuff, but I no longer doubted he would keep at it. He slipped, stumbled, and fell without quitting.

It's beautiful to see a child discover the love of craft. I felt older every time I helped him practice, ragged and proud, but I know that on my deathbed, whether I'm on it next week or manage to stick around for a few more decades, I'll think about my little boy growing into an individual of great purpose during a time of pandemic.

I suspect that for many people, those fortunate enough to survive anyway, this will be a time of intense memory. It sometimes feels like the pandemic is an existential affliction—not a mere outbreak that has disrupted the global economy, but a mutation of the world into something eerie and unknowable. Public discourse is filled with tacit anxiety that we're not returning to whatever each of us considers normal.

But normal was already a tragedy for millions of people forced to exist in conditions of pandemic—lockdown, dearth, precarity—not because of a coronavirus, but as surplus organisms, economic pathogens under capitalism. Normalcy is another kind of health crisis.

I found a kind of peace in my exertion, a childish enthusiasm for fantasies of a joyful future, an unadulterated sense of wonder heretofore overwhelmed by the pain and stress of joblessness. It emerged from the click and clack of an obstinate young boy powering through the world's artificial dips and angles. Suddenly, ebullient and dead tired, I was determined to persist until that season of the unorthodox inspired another resurrection.

■ ■ ■

The family gatherings returned as the weather improved, only this time they were outdoors. My father, in his eighties and a smoker for six decades (now quit), proclaimed that the virus would do him in if he caught it, and nobody thought he was being silly.

We normally got together at my brother's house. He has a good patio and enough of a yard to placate the children. I was never excited for these occasions. My familial relationships aren't outwardly strained, but my reclusive tendencies override my willingness to suffer the inner strain of nearly all social situations. Somebody at the table always wanted to discuss my recent job history. The habit was supposedly innocent and thoroughly repulsive. Nothing they said emerged without at least a dash of tacit judgment. They were less guarded about an obsessive concern for my near-term survival prospects. I didn't like being there. A lot of therapists stay in business with clients who feel guilty about this kind of sentiment, but to my knowledge guilt has never solved the problem from which it emerges.

I kept reminding myself, "You're doing it for your son."

But what was I really doing for him? Allowing him to watch his old man brood at an otherwise lively table? Acclimating him to passive-aggression? Inducting him into the anguish of filial obligation?

I would slip away and have a stroll. Some buses were parked at an adult learning center a few blocks away. I walked past them and wished I could start one up and barrel off in perfect loneliness. It's easy to get inside a school bus and drive off if you know what you're doing. (The only advice I'll offer is to make sure the air tanks are full enough for the brakes to work.) But I'd surely get busted. Cameras and tracking devices make school buses pretty much theft-proof. Besides, where would I go? There was nobody to pick up.

In truth, I didn't want to go anywhere. I just missed driving a bus. A part of me knew that I wasn't returning to the job for a long while, or at all, and I hated that such a critical era of my life had ended so abruptly. Every now and again, I had to do a training session or some other errand. They were joyless affairs. The county began using buses to deliver meals, but I stayed home with my son. We decided that we would return to school together. The sense of finality persisted and with each passing week metastasized into something palpable. It wouldn't have been so bad if I had other options. But bus driving was my last resort. What happens after all of a person's resorts are exhausted?

The novels. I had those, at least. They were physical assets likely worth nothing in material value, but in the luckiest timeline they were a potential source of wealth. More than money, though, they offered proof that I was doing something. I wasn't simply a lapsed academic or a bus driver with nothing to do. I was a *writer*. I had an identity. But not if I couldn't get the novels published—I could still be a writer, but not one recognized by social convention. Until that happened, I would be just another poser with a laughable dream, only much older than the usual specimen. I was terrified of being unemployed again. The moment, I admitted with dread, was already upon me.

Writing had transitioned from a source of pleasure into a preface for survival, emotionally if not financially. I produced a lot of work, three novels in two years, and went about finding a publisher. I was open to nearly all possibilities. I decided to avoid explicitly "political" outlets because I didn't want the fiction associated with my extant reputation. The actions underlying my public profile were indivisible from the work, of course, but I wasn't writing politics in fiction in the same way I do in genres more accommodating of polemics. All I had going for me was a small body of what I considered excellent work. I was a poor candidate for literary stardom.

I was on the far periphery of the creative writing industry and already understood that it was similar to academe in its insularity and inscrutability. If you're not feted as a rising star from the get-go due to pedigree or connections—or just the right kind of liberal politics, heavy on identity and barren of class—then trying to get something published is a grueling task. You either have juice or you're a nuisance.

The process would be much easier without seeing the stuff that actually does get published.

I did my due diligence and queried dozens of agents and independent houses. No bites. I sent another round of queries. Nothing. I didn't want to request favors from anyone. So I went back to the queries. Same result.

After a ton of frustration and some furious internal dialogue, I asked some people that I know for introductions. I finally spoke to a few actual human agents. It went okay, but I immediately decided that, as a professional class, agents are full of shit (and nothing since then has changed my opinion). Instead of canned rejections, I got a few personalized ones, which were much worse: querying 101 spiels and some boilerplate about how publishing works. It came across as either patronizing or perfunctory. There's something to be said for bluntness, even if it might seem brutal at first: "I don't really have time for a nobody like you"; "this shit ain't gonna sell"; "you have no talent; consider driving a large vehicle, instead." That kind of thing. Pious encouragement is incredibly demoralizing.

I wasn't surprised by my lack of success. There wasn't much a middle-aged burnout could pitch to agents and publishers. Everyone could probably sense that I had no desire to be a part of that world. I wanted to publish books; I had no interest in the culture of book publishing. My enthusiasm came upon all the wrong places.

Still, I was taken by something unquantifiable by industry standards. I loved the work—not simply as a product, but as an act of production. I wouldn't get published, in part because of my crappy attitude, but in figurative and perhaps even literal ways, the discovery of yet another failed career saved my life.

■ ■ ■

I walk down the stairwell to the basement, making sure my foot is planted firmly on each step. A few years earlier, my sock failed to grip the hardwood and I ended up on the floor with a broken computer.

I reach the bottom of the stairwell and swing around to the sliding glass door across the basement. I slip my feet into my sneakers, blue mesh Nike Revolutions from 2017, without untying them. I check my pocket for a mask. I pause to make sure I don't have to pee. I pull the toboggan lower on my ears.

Everything is in order.

I slide open the door and step into our back garden, a patch of misshapen concrete tile, brick inlay, and bedraggled lawn. It takes seven steps to reach the gate, which I latch behind me after jiggling the handle. To my left, the parking lot ends with a yellow curb that my son and I use as a makeshift soccer goal. To my right, two rows of cars stretch out for what seems like half a mile. I stroll between the cars, in the middle of the asphalt. Serotonin seeps into my frontal cortex. I start to feel more relaxed.

My son is doing his half hour of Phys Ed, so I needn't worry about him for the moment. Diana is at her normal spot at the dining room table, papers spread around her laptop in three directions. Our son will likely interrupt her work, but not for a little while longer. He generally stays locked in his exercises.

There aren't many people out. Those I do see aren't eager for conversation, so we pass with slight nods, our gazes aimed at the street. I don't use the sidewalk. There is little car traffic and I don't want to walk an arc in the soggy grass whenever anybody passes.

The surroundings are painfully consistent: townhouses pressed together in rows of six or eight, all built of brick with matching eight-foot walls. The different colors and textures don't ease the homogeneity. Parking lots are in the back. The streets curve and slope, with cars lining each side—a dizzying variety of compact sedans and midsized SUVs.

But there is prettiness to be found despite the best efforts of suburban planners. Foliage isn't inhibited by the miserable weather. A great variety of blooms fill the neighborhood: Holly, Dogwood, Japanese Maple, Crepe Myrtle. The grass has lost most of its straw color and is now the festive green so magical to anyone who remembers its sight and smell as a child.

I move toward the edge of the complex. Behind the lowest parking lot is a greenbelt surrounding a drainage creek. It has come to life with the chirping of robins and blue jays and the critters flitting among newly risen switchgrass.

The wind is in my face and I regress my head deeper into the collar of my jacket. I reach the edge of the complex and walk across a muddy lawn to the parkway running alongside it. The road is empty. Traffic has decreased throughout the region. On the other side of the parkway is a pool club and single-family houses. We figure we'll never be able to afford one, but they're nice to look at. Teardowns—destroying old houses and replacing them with McMansions—haven't yet come to our part of the county.

I walk up the parkway for a few hundred yards and then turn back into the complex. The wind now at my back, I slow my pace and examine my neighbors' yard décor. Nothing exciting. (The HOA doesn't allow excitement.) A few wreaths and ceramic animals. The occasional American flag and home security sign.

As I get near home, I see my son running toward me, an eager grin below his huge brown eyes. He jumps into me, a greeting that will never grow tiresome, despite its increasingly dubious physics.

"Papa! Let's play hide-and-seek."

"What about school?"

"We're on break."

"Well come on then."

He grabs my hand and pulls me toward the greenbelt from which I had just arrived. The world feels brighter, no matter the drizzle now coating my glasses. He is growing quickly. I remember this fact in moments of frustration. It breaks my heart and also gives me tremendous energy. I will continue walking for as long as my body allows, but the world will be slightly different every time I return—and it won't be long before nobody is at the end to greet me.

■　■　■

I couldn't grow accustomed to having no work. The masking, lockdown, sanitizing, and online shopping were eerie novelties that quickly evolved into normal reality. There was no longer a future to imagine and it was clear the past wasn't coming back.

The fear of falling ill was especially strong. My father wasn't the only one with concerns. I had a pretty poor profile as a potential COVID patient: iffy diet, a smoker, slightly overweight. A lot of pundits were saying that COVID is overhyped, but I didn't want to become an anonymous statistic that proved them wrong.

Losing my job—I hadn't been fired but had lost a job, none-theless—was especially difficult to accept. I recognized that I was fortunate—the job would eventually return, and we were still getting paid—but the psychic benefits of bus driving were more important than anything. They provided a sense of purpose and a social identity. Now I was a writer embarrassed to disclose my occupation.

I thought a lot about the people who had no respite, particularly the workers keeping the infrastructure intact and delivering food and other necessities. Eventually, I decided to do my own shopping. It didn't seem right to ask another human being to assume a risk that I wouldn't take on, no matter what kind of tip I left. I couldn't do anything for people vulnerable to household violence, which felt like a deeply inhuman condition. Their presence in the world, unseen but painfully obvious, was enough to reinforce any decent person's commitment to insurgency.

The whole situation was bizarre. Of all the ways I could have lost my latest job, a virus wasn't anything I had ever considered. I occasionally wrote about my career switch from academe to bus driving but was careful not to disclose information about my employer. Audiences would know that I worked in Northern Virginia, but it might have been any of five counties: Loudon, Prince William, Fairfax, Alexandria, or Arlington. (A discerning reader could have figured out pretty easily that it was Fairfax.)

I didn't think it a good idea to mention the county for basic reasons of propriety, but a greater concern existed. I was afraid that the same reactionary forces that had expunged me from academe would go after my new job. It sounds fanciful, but being punitive is their stock in trade. They aren't an easygoing bunch; they're quite hung up on destitution. I've learned over three decades that Zionists don't ever stop going after anyone who opposes their beloved settler colony. They had interfered with my career since I was a grad student. They dragged me to court after blacklisting me. I wouldn't give them a chance to get me fired from yet another job. I waited for the organized defamation campaign: "how can Jewish students feel safe with an antisemitic bus driver?"; "he needs a pro-Israel attendant for balance"; "Palestinians are known for blowing up buses!"

After a while, I realized that they had no intention of complaining. They were happy with where I was. My social media mentions were filled with snide, mocking comments about being a bus driver. They figured that driving a school bus was adequate humiliation. In an honest living, Zionists finally found something for which a Palestinian was suited. As far as they were concerned, I had already become destitute.

I knew it would be different in the literary world. Novels are potentially influential items. Writers are significant, respectable. I had to consider the possibility that the reactionary forces would make a stink if I managed to sell one of my manuscripts and wasn't especially confident in the willingness (or ability) of a corporate publisher to tell them to kick rocks. I tried to assure myself that I was being paranoid, that pro-Israel partisans likely don't give a damn what I do, but the concern wasn't so easy to shrug off. I was no longer dealing with a working-class formation. This was literature—high culture—an industry formed through CIA involvement and supposedly apolitical motifs. The few transgressive classics get aestheticized through the corresponding lit-crit industry. For any of these fears to matter, I'd first have to become noteworthy, so my frustrations were simultaneously a kind of salvation.

I was fretting over a hypothetical that was also totally concrete. I could well become the subject of a smear campaign, but only if I achieved a recognition constitutionally inaccessible to people of my ilk—disreputable because of the aforementioned slander. The dilemma isn't as outrageous as it sounds. For Palestinians in North America, Zionist recrimination is a fact of life. It shadows all our dreams of success. The grander the dream, the darker the shadow. We always have to prepare for snitching and defamation. It doesn't matter how likely they are to happen in any particular instance; the point is that it happens frequently enough for it to have affected our consciousness. It was something many of our parents warned about all the way back when we were in high school. Luckily, I wasn't merely a nobody in the publishing world; I was a negative entity. It's easier to create literature in that situation. Getting published is mostly a formality; if humanity survives, there will always be a reader.

I kept researching and sending query letters. I was prepared for a fight. I stay ready for the oppressor's viciousness, as a matter of principle.

Despite their belief that they took everything from me, I've been able to lead a rich, meaningful life. If driving a school bus is punishment, then I'm fortunate to have experienced the greatest carceral system ever invented. I got to hear children's laughter every morning and afternoon. I got to read at the trunk of an ancient oak tree. I got to write stories at the wheel of a magic yellow vehicle.

Among the many lessons to derive from my recent experiences, one stands out: no Zionist has ever stopped me from doing something I wanted to do. There's no reason any oppressor should stop you, either.

● ● ●

The sense of gloom persisted, interrupted by beautiful moments of filial affection. I had more time to write, I had gotten mornings back with my son, and neither godsend relieved my discontent.

Every time I drove a car, I imagined navigating as if I were on a bus. I tried to remember the pre-trip routine in random moments. My muscle memory of the bus's dashboard knobs faded and my hand came to move naturally among the car's tedious controls.

You could say that I was having some trouble accepting the changes.

Yet I was experiencing an unrecognized sense of relief. Transporting children is a source of incredible stress that I didn't fully comprehend until I noticed its absence. Too many things can happen. Things that are highly unlikely, but terrifying in their possibilities.

People like to cite stats that show car travel to be more dangerous than air travel. Why, then, are so many people afraid of flying? They must be irrational, goes the thinking. Not so. They're being quite rational, actually. Car wrecks are common, but even if you suffer one, there's only a small chance of dying. Airplanes rarely crash, but if one does crash, you're almost certainly a goner. In other words, it's not a matter of general statistics, but of specific odds.

That's how school bus driving was for me: I was well-trained and conscientious, and the chances of a horrible accident were miniscule, but the mere existence of a chance could feel unbearable.

When I was at the training center, I thought a lot about my childhood bus driver. His name was Bill Deaver. We called him Bill. No Mr. Deaver or Mr. Bill. Just Bill. He was elderly—or seemed elderly to us at the time—and spoke in a gravelly drawl. He was one of the custodians at the middle school in between his morning and afternoon shifts.

We adored Bill. He drove a Blue Bird with a company logo on the first aid compartment up by the student mirror. He would claim to keep a bluebird in the compartment and we'd beg him to open it and show us. We were pretty sure it was a fib but weren't sure enough that it could squelch our curiosity. It was the perfect ruse for youngsters, fanciful enough to trigger our skepticism, but so intriguing that it exploited our naïveté. I could never understand why Bill didn't just open the compartment and settle the debate once and for all.

He was famous for pulling teeth. I look back on the tradition with a mixture of shock and amusement. I would never dream of putting my hands anywhere near a student's mouth, but in those days, in that place, nobody seemed to mind. The parents probably figured that Bill was saving them an unpleasant task. Getting a tooth pulled by Bill was a big deal. He'd grab a tissue and start the extraction, more expertly than any dentist. As soon as we detected a loose tooth, we'd wiggle it furiously with our tongues, hoping Bill would deem it ready to come out. If it wasn't ready in the morning, the tooth would be subject to rigorous jiggling and waggling throughout the school day in the hope that it could be pulled on the ride home.

Even today, Bill's name is apt to come up in conversation among people of a certain age from Bluefield, Virginia. He was essential to our childhoods.

A handful of those people might recall Bill taking us to school on a snowy morning, sometime in the early eighties. It was unusual to have school during winter weather—it got cold and miserable in our part of the world, but it wasn't quite the Yukon—so I don't remember (and can't imagine) the circumstances that would've had us on a school bus during an accumulating snowfall. Usually an inch was enough to keep us home.

Whatever the reason, we were sent to school, probably excited as all hell because of the awful weather. Bill started his route in my neighborhood, a two-block subdivision with forty houses. He drove around from the other side and by the time he got to my stop, across the street from my driveway, there would have been about eight kids on the bus. On that morning, I could hear the tire chains jingling before the bus appeared over the hill. (I learned how to put on the chains by easing the inner back tires onto wooden blocks, but newer buses can do it automatically.)

My mom waited with me and my brother. A child of the tropics, she was paranoid about driving in the snow. My dad, on the other hand, was completely at ease. It snowed every now and then in Jordan, but nobody would call the Levant a winter climate. Dad had been gone for an hour already and so Mom was in charge of extracting reassurance from the bus driver.

She had a real fresh-off-the-boat sensibility and an exotic physiognomy—in other words, she was unmistakably foreign—but she adored Bill and, befitting an aging Appalachian, he responded to her as a consummate gentleman. Every Christmas, and at the end of the school year, mom would load him down with baked goods. Baklava usually, which was a rare dessert in Appalachia at the time.

"They was mighty good, Mrs. Salaita," he would say in a lazy baritone, pronouncing "Salaita" in the local dialect: Suh-lot-uh.

My brother and I boarded the bus and mom stuck her head in behind us to ask if the roads were okay.

"Well, they're a bit rough this morn," Bill explained.

"Please be careful."

"Will do."

After scooping me and my brother, the bus went to a larger subdivision called Pinehill Park. Between the two subdivisions were a golf course and a small pond flowing into the town's water treatment system. We often walked there in the afternoon to feed the ducks and clamber around the large rocks where the pond narrowed into a stream. A narrow road ran alongside the pond, with a ridge on the other side. That stretch of road had some intense curves.

As Bill neared the scariest one, just before a small bridge the town would shut down years later, the bus fishtailed and ended up in a ditch, its right side resting against the face of the ridge. I don't remember anyone screaming, although it almost certainly must have happened. Bill made his way down the aisle. Nobody was injured. The cops showed up and blocked the street. Mom came along shortly thereafter, loud and frantic. She had seen the police lights from our living room.

With the help of the cops (and my mom), Bill managed to inch the bus forward enough to open the door. Other parents had turned up by then, fussing over us as if we'd just emerged from a well.

Bill kept running a hand through his dusty silver hair, now frazzled, and apologizing to the police and parents. Everyone reassured him that he shouldn't feel bad, but Bill wasn't buying it. He looked at the ground, defeated and despondent.

But Bill had only endeared himself to us even more. We were getting to miss school and he might have been responsible for closing down the entire county.

It would take me over thirty years to properly recognize Bill's pain in that moment. Adulthood only comes into focus as a constant reassessment of earlier memories. Once I began carting around children, I could understand Bill's defeated expression beyond the visceral, as something palpably and physically unnerving. Even after I stopped driving, the fear never went away.

■ ■ ■

"Okay, I have one," I announce. "Big Mac or Whopper?"

"Big Mac," they yell in unison.

I decide to push back. "I'm not sure, the Whopper is more filling, I think." It doesn't matter that I've eaten neither burger in years. I need an argument and the one I just raised seems reasonable.

"Yeah, but it still doesn't taste better," the kid right behind me says.

He has me there. We were debating flavor, not volume.

We play the same game every morning. Which is better. Who is cooler. Would you rather. Dominos or Papa John's? Krispy Kreme or Dunkin Donuts? Barca or Madrid? Apple or PC? Lebron or Jordan?

(It's a less acrimonious version of the game adult leftists play incessantly. Marx or Bakunin? Kautsky or Lenin? Deng or Mao? Stalin or Trotsky? Chomsky or Parenti?)

These students are in the Advanced Academic Program—the latest term for gifted and talented—and so they attend a school outside their home district. One elementary and middle school in any given area offers AAP and the county is obliged to provide students with transportation. Those routes generally aren't desirable. They require a lot of driving, which in turn requires more frequent trips to the pump. Filling up can take over half an hour depending on the line. On the good side, there aren't many AAP students, so the bus generally isn't unruly.

I was in the same type of program for a while in third or fourth grade before they kicked me out for insubordination. I refused to do additional assignments. My parents were furious, but I suppose over the years they grew accustomed to my revulsion at any sort of exceptionalism, especially if it requires extra work.

This route has a total of six students, five boys and a girl who rarely speaks. But if the which-or-which question is compelling, she'll pipe up with an answer. It's weird to drive a full-sized bus with only a few passengers gathered at the front, but I'm no longer in the business of questioning management. The county tells me where to drive and I do it. One of the kids always stands in the seat behind me and I constantly have to tell him to sit. It feels like we're in an Impala or Town Car from the 1970s.

One morning, I drive the final stretch to the elementary school, ready to drop off the kids and take my break. We move through the main artery of a residential neighborhood, and even though I don't have to stop, the driver behind the bus is getting impatient. I can see him gesticulating from my side mirror. No matter. The universal bus driver attitude toward irritable little cars is a shrug and a fuck you. But then the asshole decides to pass the bus. Cars are parallel parked on both sides of the street. The driver has a dangerous understanding of geometry. He persists, anyway, and I get a middle finger once he's pulled even with me. I check if the kids have noticed. They seem oblivious. Good. I'm calm, but if they saw the gesture I would've been pissed off.

On cue, a car comes from the other direction. The nincompoop passing me doesn't have time to clear the bus, so he speeds up and tries to get in front of me. I lurch right, but there's little space and I'm mindful of the time I popped a rearview mirror in a similar situation. I slam the brakes and we all lunge forward. The bus is only a few inches from the parked cars. I apply the emergency brake and turn around in my seat.

"Are you okay?" I ask, trying to keep my voice calm. They're okay. They barely noticed. "Ferrari or Lamborghini?" one of them asks.

But I'm not okay.

"Ferrari," I say. "That one's easy."

The kids disagree. They like the Lambo's gaudiness.

I was never much of a car guy, but in this moment I'd prefer any vehicle to the one their parents have entrusted me to drive.

■ ■ ■

Whatever stress I derived from school bus driving was replaced by the kind of stress that school bus driving mitigated. The stress of writing is harder to tamp down. Much of it arises from external factors—pitching ideas and finding publishers mainly, but also constant variations of routine. It's a less innocent form of stress.

Lockdown didn't mean that we were always home, but we were always together. I kept my laptop open when I wasn't in the kitchen or monitoring my son's at-home schooling. In addition to being a caretaker, I was his playmate, the peculiar upshot of having an only child. During breaks and after school, I needed to entertain him and we spent hours with his toys and tearing about the outdoors, or simply watching television.

He had grown so much since our return from Beirut in 2017. He was unusually tall, well over five feet by age seven. But he was a little boy, lean and lanky, the cherubic markings of childhood still evident in his cheek structure. Sometimes people reacted to him as if he were a teenager because of his height. Sometimes his own parents failed to adequately distinguish physical and emotional maturity.

My impatience at the constant interruptions of home life made me feel rotten. Flaws can sit so heavily on the consciousness that one feels too weak to remove them. I gave it a try, but usually surrendered to punishing exertion.

It was a wonderful and frightening thing to witness my son's developing sense of perception. As a parent, you understand that children absorb everything, even—or especially—stuff the parent considers undetectable or insignificant. But when the children become capable of reading back parental behavior, the understanding is no longer abstract. It's a very real and momentous affirmation of a parent's tremendous responsibility.

My son had begun to notice body language and expression. He intuited surroundings as adeptly as ever, but suddenly he had developed a sophisticated processing mechanism and could react to parental energy with his own lexical and physical vocabulary. Despite my own childlike recognitions, I had underestimated his ability to absorb my stress.

Although he was growing, neither of us could let go of our nightly ritual. We would stretch side by side on his bed with a book—a lot of Encyclopedia Brown and the wimpy kid's diary in those days—and take turns reading aloud. After a few pages, he would become sleepy and rest his head in the groove between my shoulder and pec. I would do all the reading from that point on.

We were in that pose one evening when he glanced at me with a timid expression. It had been one of those restless days. He had no kids to play with and I was trying to finish an essay. Every half hour he dragged me to the basement to kick a soccer ball or smash up matchbox cars. Reluctantly, I obliged. Few things destroy me more than a child's loneliness. He must have been processing the day's events as I read.

"Papa?"

"Yes, darling?"

"I'm sorry I annoy you."

■ ■ ■

I eventually figured out the nature of my anxiety during lockdown. I suspect it was a communal anxiety, the outcome of a society in a state of insignificance. Everyone kept pining for a return to normalcy, before remembering the misery inherent to the life of a normal citizen in the United States. Nobody was a do-gooder anymore. Nobody was rescuing or redeeming a broken democracy. We had no polity to smooth our flaws, no exceptional ideals to believe in. We were forced into apostasy. The civilizational decline was suddenly empirical. My radical perspective was no longer deviant. I stopped being a stranger to the rest of the country. It was an unexpected confluence that further eroded my perception of linear time. I was aware of experiencing future memories in real time; I knew that if I reached old age I would look back at the joy and tension with my family through a magically sanitized nostalgia, and so those imagined sketches of the future became superimposed onto the present. They consigned me to perpetual regret. I would yearn for the very frustration I wanted to escape. It was another world, a never-world, an obscure world defined by always-impending sadness that easily overwhelmed precarious gestures of happiness. Everywhere was a sort of fuzzy nonexistence, a worldly geography concretely defined by incoherence. I had long thought-sessions about offing myself—a logical solution, I felt, to professional desolation, for dying is more often honest than living—but even this simple possibility proved incredibly complicated: I couldn't allow my little boy, this eager and beautiful and increasingly self-aware turbine of wonderment and affection and sincerity, to believe that he was in any way annoying.

Now a one-income family again, the exorbitant cost of life in the DC suburbs became more worrisome. We were never good with money, preferring spontaneity to budgeting, so the loss of my salary, despite its meagerness, stressed our finances. I continued on as a stay-at-home dad and was pretty useful in the role, but it produced a nagging ambivalence. It was profoundly satisfying and persistently tedious all at once. Gone were airports and ballrooms, replaced by baseball gloves and grilled cheese sandwiches. I didn't want to miss the excitement of public life, but moments of nostalgia crept into my brain, anyway. I walked to the grocery store almost every day, packed lunch for my son, attempted exotic recipes, and puttered around the house looking for something interesting to consider. I drafted social media posts and sat on a folding chair along with other parents at soccer practice, neck deep in windbreakers. I was a responsible citizen of a vibrant non-society. I remember the sense of desperation more than anything. Something needs to change, I kept telling myself. Something, goddammit, anything. But for anything to happen, everything needed to change.

From Alexandria to Cairo

Online forms can be deathly tedious. This one was worse than most. It wanted lots of information already available on the CV that I was required to upload. University attendance, with enrollment and graduation dates. Dissertation topic. Recent publications. Then there was the bevy of personal stuff, including race and religion.

It was a task I never thought I would do again. The newness of a familiar process made it all the more arduous. I was both saddened and amused to see the same old redundancy. Why in the world do you need my referees' addresses? Didn't you already make me provide their emails and phone numbers? Are you planning to send them a fucking letter?

I reviewed my entries carefully, either because of old age or a brand-new sense of decorum. I don't know. For once, the idea of typos and lazy answers bothered me. I had already decided that I wouldn't half-ass the process. I would put forth maximal effort or sit it out altogether. I gave the form another read through. I checked my Word files three times before uploading them. Everything seemed to be on the up-and-up.

I hit send and went downstairs for a cigarette.

■ ■ ■

Here's what I've been trying to say for over a hundred pages: memoir is basically a futile attempt to transform variable self-images into something permanent. The memoirist picks and chooses substance from a vast set of content, just like a journalist or teacher. Truth and objectivity aren't the same. The final product has been heavily mediated by conscious or implicit selection. A story—coherent, optimally—emerges from a surfeit of raw material. The rest is discarded or restricted to assumption and suggestion.

Experience doesn't exist in a vacuum. As such, the genre is attached to events and settings. Circumstances produce the memoirist. We write and read in states of immensity.

I could have fluffed up this book with a bunch of autobiographical factoids, but I can't imagine they would interest anyone; they provide no basis for connection, in any case. Mention of my hometown might flatter somebody from Bluefield; my college would elicit a groan or smile from somebody who went to Radford; my taste in music could maybe provide the illusion of a psychic or emotional connection. But illusive connections make for a shallow reading experience. I maintain hope that we can connect at a revolutionary level.

In the end, I'm nothing more than a nexus of untold convergences. Factoids are incidental. Anecdotes and observations are my entire autobiography.

I really would have liked to include some gossip and debauchery, if only to ease the reader's suffering, but they weren't viable options. Gossip is essentially a lowbrow version of social critique, so, in a sense, I've already done a whole lot of gossiping. Which specific people did I have in mind? I don't know. Think of somebody who matches the description of a general criticism and there's your answer.

And despite a negative reputation in some corners, I have no luridness to confess. My vices, as I said, are nicotine and THC. Otherwise, I try to stay away from the world. There was a time when I gave lots of speeches. I was in dozens of different cities and never did any carousing. My hotel beds were empty, just me and a laptop with the TV on for background noise. At bars and restaurants—places I was dragged to as part of each visit—I ordered water. If I wanted to get crazy, I'd ask for a lemon wedge. On nights that I was especially parched from hours of yammering and glad-handing, I allowed myself a Coke.

All in all, I'm quite boring. It's not easy to write a memoir based on that quality.

At the same time, there's something exciting about submitting dullness to public scrutiny. It shows that in our most vulnerable moments we're all boring in the exact same way. Vulnerability, then, can be something of a social contract. I embrace that version of it, anyway.

When I first became notorious, people related to me as a symbol. I don't blame them. There was no other way to know me, aside from personal interaction. That's the nature of being a public figure. I can't say that I liked it, but I didn't spend much time worrying about something I couldn't change. I was bothered, though, by those who predicated support on my conformity. A lot of people had tacit (and at times explicit) demands about what kind of person I ought to be, or ought to become. They could be vicious if I declined the overture. (That, too, is the nature of being a public figure.) Such demands had a lot to do with my dislike of notoriety. Regarding a public figure as a symbol is one thing. Demanding the fealty of a stranger is a different kind of problem, as is expecting all interplay, even the impersonal kind, to be transactional.

I still feel a sharp pang of sorrow when remembering a common rebuke: "and to think, I supported you!"

Almost always, the rebuke was predicated on a rejection of liberalism: I had criticized Hillary Clinton; I had declined to sound like a think tank functionary; I had expressed a dim view of voting in the United States. I think some people had a difficult time believing that I'm legitimately radical. Or a difficult time understanding what radicalism actually entails.

And so I decided early in this project that writer and reader wouldn't develop an antagonistic relationship. Some readers will hate me, no doubt. That's okay (though, to be completely honest, I'm cool if you feel like keeping it to yourself). I don't mean uniformity of reaction. I'm speaking to a baseline of mutual respect in the spirit of Peter Tosh's "I Am That I Am":

> I'm not in this world
> To live up to your expectations
> Neither are you here to live up to mine, yeah
> I don't owe no one
> No obligation

No, I don't mean none
So everything is fine, fine

In short, we aren't here to enforce conformity. The only thing I have to offer is an honest story. Your humanity is the only thing I will accept in return.

• • •

I can have a hard time shutting up when the topic of notoriety arises. (I suppose you could also call it fame or infamy, but I'm not sure that widespread recognition in a very small community qualifies anyone to be famous.)

A lot of my difficulties arise from the fallout of public controversy. Psychological difficulty, mainly, although there have been problems with money and instability. We're told to unpack our issues, but sometimes there's too much clutter for the available space. So we talk and talk without a satisfying resolution. Often the circumstances producing the difficulties don't change. We unpack a set of issues and the world promptly restocks them.

I think that of all the jobs I ever had, unpublished novelist is my least favorite (this includes working for tips at a place called Texas Steakhouse and Saloon). I hated writing without knowing if the material would ever see the light of day. I contented myself with the understanding that the work exists, it will outlive me, and perhaps it might someday be of use to my son. I reminded myself that I had spent a lifetime rejecting the temporary pleasure of petty rewards and focused on the pleasures of textual permanence. Still, I didn't like having a job contingent on the permission of cultural elites or social media tastemakers. This problem seems more and more common under late-stage capitalism.

Raising a child and writing books were supposed to be meaningful and yet both could feel incredibly alienating. Life was filled with unfathomable ambiguities. I could be profoundly satisfied and in the next instant restless and disaffected. I came to understand these vacillations as the normal social life of unemployment. Working outside the formal economy, as a domestic obligation or simply for the pursuit of joy, comes with built-in ostracism. You can always see pity or reproach in people's eyes. It's hard to even make small talk without a job that others recognize as legitimate, never mind dealing with the anguished nattering of immigrant parents.

In this sense, bus driving was a godsend. The job got my family health insurance and a wage, both badly needed, but it also offered a rare sense of belonging. I recoiled when people portrayed my move from academe to the school bus as a fall from grace or a kind of tragedy. I never saw it that way. The circumstances of that move were unfortunate, no doubt, and underlain by a hint of despair. But the change itself was rather conventional. It was a public story, that's all, and so it needed a theme. Personal downfall is always a solid choice.

The situation is difficult to talk about, even in a memoir. I'm not sure how to do it without sounding narcissistic or self-congratulatory. In the end, I did what was necessary in order to hold on to a few beliefs that I consider nonnegotiable. This too is typical human behavior. I think that my story generated so much interest because it evokes a common fear among academics of being left without a job and inadequate training for anything else. (Things are changing, slowly, but for most students in the humanities and social sciences, grad school provides training specifically for academe, and the acquired skills can feel suffocatingly provincial.) My situation speaks to widespread precariousness and insecurity within the profession. A lot of academics fear that they're a half step from indigence. For the precarious, I embody a particular kind of worry.

I also embody a particular kind of fantasy: the person who said, "fuck this" and found a simpler way of living. Not quite a noble savage trope but drawing from a certain romance about old-fashioned grit and industriousness (which my own writing has probably fed into). It's better than being seen as destitute, I suppose. The only perception I embrace is that of a person who refused to concede in the face of institutional hostility. I'm proud of that refusal.

Observers can grow attached to their image of public figures. I'm always one unpopular comment away from squandering my credibility. Most romance isn't long term, after all.

But really, who knows? I may well be talking a whole lot of nonsense.

In the end, I can't say whether I'm pleased or unhappy with how it all happened. I know that I'm not regretful and have never thought about moderating my politics for access or upward mobility. Beyond that, it's up to whatever audience remains to make sense of my professional troubles, as suits their predilections. I'll only say that I never liked the idea of my life as a cautionary tale. (*The Chronicle of Higher Education* actually titled a piece that it reprinted from my website "My Life as a Cautionary Tale." It was a strange lesson to derive from the essay that followed, which was about the healing properties of defiance.) As I see it, as I experienced it, choosing to drive a bus was an affirmation of freedom. So many people—at times, myself included—tacitly reinforced the idea of driving as lesser work, as an existential downgrade, as inappropriate for a former professor, which only validated academe's exceptional self-image. There was nothing tragic about becoming a bus driver. The tragedy exists in the ghoulish culture of higher education.

■ ■ ■

One low point from that period stands out. I was about a month out of the training center, driving my own route, when a bunch of important stuff stopped working all at once. I likewise began running out of my anti-anxiety medication. It didn't require a prescription in Beirut and so I stocked up on it before returning to the United States, knowing I wouldn't have insurance. Whole pills became half pills and soon I was dividing each pill into quarters. I could feel my brain straining for a proper dose.

Then my code for the government gas pump started failing. I would later learn that it's a pretty common occurrence, but at the time it caused me great panic. We're not supposed to let our tanks go below half (although plenty of drivers took theirs much closer to E) and I was good about following the rule. For starters, I wasn't keen on inhaling diesel fumes for fifteen minutes. I'm one of those weirdos who likes the aroma of burning diesel, but it smells disgusting coming out of the pump.

One morning, when I tried to top off just below three-quarters the computer wouldn't grant me access. No biggie. Must be some glitch. I tried again the next day. Same problem. By that point I was getting annoyed. Refueling cuts into break time. When the same thing happened a third time, after PM shift, I called it in. Dispatch informed me that they'd have to contact Fuel Force, the supplier, between the hours of nine and five. It was 5:05.

So I headed in early the following morning with the idea that I could tinker with the system without the pressure of a line behind me. Nothing worked. I knew dispatch would tell me to try later, but I radioed in, anyway. The channel was empty so I could haggle a bit. The dispatcher told me to wait until nine. Her tone was categorical. There would be no haggling.

I waited around for AM runs to begin, hotboxing cigarettes and slowly working my brain chemicals into a simmer. My tank was creeping down to a quarter. I wondered if the old shitbox even had a low fuel light. I finished morning shift and headed toward the pump—yes, in the singular—wishing I had a full complement of crazy powder in my system instead of the nub of a pill I had ingested that morning. As usual for that time of day, the line was long. I waited my turn, knowing that I'd have to call in the problem. At least I was there during business hours.

I pulled up next to the pump and punched my code into the machine. Rejected. I hopped back onto the bus and grabbed the radio mic. By that point, I figured the entire county knew about my problem. Dispatch told me to wait ten minutes and then try the pump again. I glanced in the mirror at the line of buses behind me. I had no other choice. I was on the verge of resolving a serious problem.

Soon enough, I saw somebody approaching from the passenger-side mirror. It was one of the senior members of my team. I signaled for him to pull open the door.

"Am I gonna be getting any gas today?"

I tried to explain my predicament, but his expression remained unhappy. "It'll only be a minute or two," I finished.

"Dispatcher said ten minutes."

"Yeah. Like I said, it won't be long."

He shook his head and stormed off.

I was left with a tremendous sense of confusion. Would I be in the right to shrug and let him stay mad? What was the protocol for gas pump hijinks? The situation had never come up during training. Feeling at least a dozen angry eyes fixated on my bus, I did something I never would have considered as a professor: give in to the will of the majority. I started the bus and looped around to the back of the line. Forty minutes later I was back, exhausted and angry. After punching in my code, I almost wept when the computer told me to begin pumping. My relief was short lived. By the time I returned to the lot, my break was more than half over. I sped home and fell asleep in an armchair with a bowl of smoked almonds on my lap.

Finding a doctor on short notice proved difficult. Everyone was scheduling out two or three months for new patients. I finally had health insurance, but no actual medical care, which struck me as a uniquely American dilemma. The last of my pills would be gone within a week and already the adverse effects were apparent. The dilemma made for a below-average nap.

I woke in the nick of time to make my afternoon shift and finished the day in a haze. On the way home, I felt the car bobbing and lurching after exiting the interstate. I knew the tire was flat. I drove home, anyway.

High on the glory of my newfound mechanical expertise, I decided to change the tire myself. My son wanted to accompany me, of course, so I showed him where the spare and jack are stored, giving a quick explanation of the tools' function. Then we laid down on the asphalt next to the tire. I figured it would be a nice memory—working on a car with his old man and all that.

I found the notch for the jack and began lifting the car (I was still driving my mom's 2006 Buick Lacrosse). Before getting it too far off the ground, I double-checked that the jack was stable. I had put it in the right spot. Unbeknownst to me, though, the underside of the old sedan was rusted. The jack pushed through the metal and the chassis landed square on the ring finger of my right hand. I want to say that I yelped, but I think it was more of a tortured groan. My son had jumped to his feet and was staring down in horror. I tried to keep collected, but I was so shocked that I had trouble focusing.

"Go get your mother," I managed to say.

With the help of a neighbor, and with my son whimpering at Diana's hip, we freed my hand. The car's underside had landed just below the fingernail. There was surprisingly little blood, but the skin surrounding the nail was mashed into a weird shape, bright red and trending toward purple. A few moments later, some paramedics showed up, but I declined to go to the hospital. Diana pointed out that a doctor could probably excuse me from work for a day or two, but I had no intention of missing any time. I was new to the job and determined to make a strong impression. It seemed like bad form to start going absent within the first month, no matter how legitimate. Besides, I knew my finger wasn't broken, just badly bruised. I had been extremely lucky.

I was profoundly embarrassed, though. Between the disastrous attempt at changing a tire and the depleted brain medicine, not to mention three days of gas pump drama, I was begging the gods for better days.

Things only got worse when it occurred to me that I could have just let down the jack and pulled my finger away.

■ ■ ■

The high point of driving wasn't a specific event or period; it was getting the children home every afternoon and then going to see my own child. You'll never find anything in academe lovelier and more life-affirming than elderly couples picking up their grandchildren from the school bus stop. It was, without question, my favorite part of the job. Another highlight was picture day, when the elementary kids stepped onto the bus all dapper and dolled up, alternately bashful and beaming with pride.

I realize that my observation about a lovely and life-affirming episode on the job may come across as smug, as an insult to those who toil in academe with great warmth and devotion. I don't mean it that way. I suppose I'm trying to say that it's good to remember the timeless gestures of love systematically beaten out of us in so many professional industries. Some of the nicest rewards aren't considered rewarding based on the typical perceptions of a successful career.

The phenomenon of grandparents picking up children from the bus, common in Northern Virginia, points to a million underlying problems. Parents are working, possibly divorced or absent. Child-care is prohibitively expensive and something that the government refuses to provide. The elderly are therefore tasked with domestic labor (and sometimes conscripted into the workforce, as well). Such a beautiful scene is also indicative of brute economic dysfunction. But these problems don't change the spontaneous delight arising in that moment of connection. The child is giddy and energized, hopping down the steps and sprinting into an embrace. The grandparent's weathered face takes on a youthful glow; all hardships of past and present are momentarily gone, replaced by a flash of bliss that transcends the ages. Then the parties clasp hands and walk away, fueled by the lingering effects of this singular experience. It is periodically regenerative fuel for the driver, as well.

So the low points of driving weren't much more than tense or disquieting inconveniences, usually brought about by fatigue and the stress of acting as caretaker to rambunctious children.

(In case you were wondering: Diana managed to find me a doctor's appointment, the local garage towed the car and had a new tire on it the same evening that it went flat, and my finger eventually returned to its original shape, although it hurt for about a week every time I popped or pushed the emergency brake.)

The high points, on the other hand, are timeless and universal, as readily comprehensible to four-year-olds as to twentysomethings and octogenarians. That's what we miss in notions of workplace pragmatism. There's a primal beauty to be found in most kinds of labor. Problem is the profit motive has rendered beauty unproductive. No matter which version of a just society you push, formal valuations of tenderness and compassion should be central to its economic calculations.

■ ■ ■

The Arab World is blessed with interesting cities. It has grand historical capitals like Baghdad, Damascus, and Cairo; coastal gems like Casablanca, Tunis, Jedda, and Aden; avatars of Orientalist fantasy like Algiers, Luxor, Tangier, and Jerusalem.

But Beirut…Beirut may well be singular. Perhaps only Alexandria can match its splendor and complexity. There's no easy way to describe the city—and even then it depends on which part of the city you have in mind, down to the specific street. Heterodox experience is its only universal feature. The city somehow feels detached from time itself. It's the kind of place where you often have a nagging suspicion that you're wandering around an elaborate film set.

The city is dirty, crowded, and often dysfunctional. It alternates between charm and aggression, pleasure and frustration, wealth and privation. It is thoroughly Lebanese, but also a hub of Armenian, Palestinian, and Syrian cultures. You can say a million things about Beirut; the only comment that others might agree with is that there's nothing like it. Hundreds of Western travelers, including Mark Twain, have written about the city. Before Lebanon's recent troubles (whose origin is subject to passionate disagreement), Western journalists liked visiting Beirut and writing startled paeans to its chicness and modernity. The stories were always silly, but also tacitly sinister in that they inevitably ignored poverty and imperialism. They celebrated an upper-class lifestyle amenable to moneyed tourists and local tycoons and inaccessible to the great majority of Beirut's actual residents. The authors clearly discovered something magical in Beirut but didn't know what to do with it.

We were there for two years, a time of intense memories. I scarcely remember anything to do with work. When Beirut comes to mind, I'm filled with images of the bus running up and down the corniche; hanging out on balconies with friends and favorite students; rare and special days at Sporting with my son. We discovered a rooftop pool in Hamra during our final summer and a banyan tree on campus, sprawling down a hillside for more than a dozen meters. We rented a car and drove down to Melita, the museum of the resistance, and drank tamarind juice on the café's massive terrace. We jumped from table-like rocks into the Mediterranean and let the current swish us back and forth.

During winter break of my second year, I developed a nagging toothache. After I realized it wasn't going away on its own, I decided to get it checked out. I'd heard good things about a dentist up on Sadat Street and paid him a visit. He was a jolly, youngish man with the kind of confidence you want in a person putting power tools in your mouth. He checked me out and recommended Panadol. I followed his instructions and returned two days later with the same problem. He checked me out again and suggested a root canal. You can never tell when one of those things is really needed, but I would have done anything to get rid of the toothache.

"I would consider that," I said.

"It's expensive," he warned.

"How much?"

"Two hundred dollars," he said grandly.

I paid him cash on the spot.

The dentist did the root canal in increments. For about an hour he'd perform violence against my tooth, stick a cap on the damage, and tell me to come back the next day. I dutifully marched up the hundred-some steps from lower campus to Hamra and faced the punishment. In the final stretch, over the course of two days—maybe it was one, I don't completely remember—he executed a series of grunting exertions and proclaimed my tooth healed. Since I had paid him up front, I could hop out of the chair and leave, my favorite thing about the arrangement.

When I returned to Virginia, I scheduled a cleaning with my sister-in-law, a dentist, and asked her about the root canal as she looked over my x-rays.

"He did a great job," she told me.

After that last appointment, I could feel half my mouth throbbing behind the lidocaine but didn't return to lower campus. Diana had told me that she was probably taking our son out to eat. I walked one block up Sadat to Hamra Street, the neighborhood's main thoroughfare and perhaps the Levant's most famous commercial area. It was cold and drizzling and a light mist emerged from my mouth with every breath. A block away was the restaurant where I figured I'd find my family.

It was called Crepaway, an American-style, sit-down chain with the usual fare, plus crepes, and the Hamra location sat on a corner and had a curved picture window. I approached the restaurant, and there were my wife and toddler, sitting next to one another at a round top in our usual nook, giggling and pointing at a menu. Diana's hair shined in the restaurant's gaudy light, dark brown with loping curls. Our son's hair was the same, only shorter. His magnificent round eyes were the same as hers. They were enchanting, almost otherworldly, sitting behind the glass as if isolated from the traumas everywhere present on my side of the window. It was like walking toward the kind of safety that every bullied child dreams about.

I practically skipped the rest of the way and once inside ran to hug both of them. It's the most wonderful memory I have of that difficult, exquisite city.

■ ■ ■

There are two Alexandrias in Virginia. One is an independent city/county abutting the Potomac and the other is a swath of Fairfax County, the informal Alexandria. I drove for a team located in the Alexandrian portion of the county. Many routes would take buses to the very edge of the county or into Alexandria city before looping back around. It was a challenging place to drive, filled with busy thoroughfares and crowded residential streets. When I began substituting, I found that the more suburban routes were decidedly easier, in both road space and student behavior.

My team served neighborhoods comprised of Northern Virginia's working class, a largely immigrant demographic. Some fancy neighborhoods were threaded in, but by and large the area didn't have a stellar reputation. Central America, East Africa, Afghanistan, the Philippines, the Middle East. Those were the main agglomerations. The kids on the bus were loud and rambunctious and wonderful.

We spent most afternoons playing language games. I supplied some common Arabic terms and learned how to say "sit down" in Amharic, Pashto, and Tagalog. I wove some sentences together in Spanish and laughed as the Salvadoran and Guatemalan kids impatiently corrected me. Sometimes I misspoke on purpose, just to raise their dander. We had a running exercise where we tried to identify all the Spanish words of Arabic origin. It would have required a field trip to West Virginia to run out of examples.

Sometimes, I still try to apply my limited Arabic to bus parts and roadside sites. I did better with an audience. If any of the parents were upset that their children were learning a crude Arabic vocabulary, none of them said anything to me about it. They were an easygoing bunch in general. On the third day of a new school year, I missed my first turn off of Route 236, not more than a hundred yards from Alexandria's border, and found myself with seventy-five elementary school children to be deposited at three stops. I took the next right, but working backward around the block wasn't going to help. The county was firm about it: no letting off students on the wrong side of the street unless it's a designated stop. So I drove past three groups of confused parents, the children screaming at them from the windows. I found no place to turn the bus in the right direction, so back around the block we went, the confusion and screaming more pronounced this time. Before the third go-around—for if anything I was an above-average study—I found a parking lot and managed to maneuver around in the right direction. I opened the door at each stop to befuddled parents and delirious passengers. One man, who had already befriended me with chitchat the first two days, stuck his head in the door.

"Steve! Where in the world were you going?"

I tried to explain my thinking. The more I talked, the more his mouth curved into a one-sided smile.

"So drop them off on the wrong side. What's the big deal?"

"The county would have my ass if I did that."

He chuckled and spread his arms. "Don't worry, Steve, we won't tell on you."

I could see by his amused expression that he was being funny but wasn't joking. It was a tremendous gesture of confidence, solidarity even, one I don't think I ever experienced in the snitch-friendly confines of academe. As I drove home that evening, it occurred to me how much social reconditioning I still needed to do. *Of course* these parents wouldn't complain about the kids being dropped off on the wrong side of the street. There wasn't a Ken or Karen in the bunch. They would think it ludicrous that crossing a street in suburban DC is some perilous event. They probably think a lot of the rules that Americans like to be uptight about are ludicrous.

And the kids, well, the kids would never know about these rules. They're governed by an entirely different legal code. In their minds, I was either playing a silly joke or just plain crazy when I zipped past their waiting parents. They were completely artless like that, and I loved them for it.

They allowed me to discover that the ideal isn't to find a labor of love, but to find love in our labor. The discovery came from dozens of simple intimacies: showing me their loose teeth, gathering around my seat for fist bumps and high fives, teaching me to speak in new languages. I hope they too grow with those memories. I surely miss them.

■ ■ ■

"I'm excited about going, but it feels different than Beirut," I said to Diana.

She smiled. "It's a different country."

"Ha ha."

We were discussing a wholly unexpected development.

"Here's the thing," I said, "I've been thinking about something . . . weird, kind of morbid. But I can't get it out of my head."

She motioned for me to continue.

"I don't know, it's just different now. Ignatius was three when we went to Beirut. He's almost ten now. Back then I had energy to travel and give talks and shit like that. Now you have to chain me to a taxi to get me to the airport."

"Sure, but this is all regular aging. It's not that different."

I sighed and got to the point. "I'm worried that we'll leave and our parents will start to die."

"Yes. That's almost certainly going to happen."

■ ■ ■

The pandemic began to wane, at least in the country's imagination, and the children returned to school. I considered getting back into the seat. Diana was opposed to the move. She had a decent job and plenty needed to be done in the house: getting our son ready for school and picking him up afterward; carting him to piano and soccer practice; putting a decent meal on the table. Being able to stay home with him was a rare luxury, she argued. I had no good counterargument. Restlessness was compelling but lacked any sense of practicality.

With the school bus driver shortage a serious motivating factor, I knew it would be near-impossible to return as a sub. The county needed full-time drivers willing to pick up extra runs every week—and I was pretty certain that unwillingness wouldn't be an option. There would be no writing or mornings with my son.

I started researching other possibilities: Fairfax Connector, Metrobus, and a few other local companies. Without a publisher, I couldn't conceive of writing novels as work. It was appropriate to view it as a living, but the labor was necessarily alienating. I wanted a job that didn't exist simply as a tax break. I also wanted to continue my domestic obligations and be around to guide my son through adolescence. Like nearly all workers under capitalism, I was faced with a choice that broached no compromise.

One lazy afternoon while waiting to pick up my son from school, I decided to check the academic job ads. I hadn't done it in about three or four years, and I have no idea what activated my curiosity. It appeared entirely random, although I consider instinctiveness and randomness to be rhetorical shorthand for complex phenomena. I suppose I had been reading so much about the miserable job market that I wanted to see for myself, find some company among other castaways consigned to economic surplus. And perhaps on some level, one I was loath to recognize, I anxiously sought an escape valve.

Starting with international ads, as I did, was a pretty good indication that I was prepared to be intrigued, for the domestic job market was a nonstarter for somebody like me, tainted by the eternal stain of controversy.

I didn't get past the first ad that I saw.

There it was, number one of eleven matches for my search: a position at the American University in Cairo which I might as well have written myself. Immediately, I was elated and profoundly regretful. I paused to think things through and landed on a single conclusion about which I was shockingly certain: if I chose to apply, I would get the job.

But did I even want to return to academe? What would it mean for my sense of place in the world? Even if I decided to return, was I willing to do it in Egypt?

Most pressing of all: was I even capable anymore?

I hadn't taught a college course in five years. I made no effort to publish according to academic models of productivity. I let my membership in professional associations lapse. I quit doing public events, except for the rare opportunity that promised meaningful engagement. I still had some friends in the industry, but otherwise I burned my bridges—not actively, mind you, but simply by dropping out of view. (Visibility is a big thing in academe.)

It would be inaccurate to say that I had become invisible—I still tweeted and posted essays to my website; some of those essays got a lot of traffic—but I was certainly making an effort to be low-key on my way to a more reclusive existence. I declined to appear on podcasts with large audiences and said no to panels with well-known colleagues. Why? I'm not sure, exactly. I didn't trust any of those people and distrust inevitably leads to isolation. (Nor should I trust such people, I maintain. I don't sell subscriptions for myself and didn't want to be used by anyone else for that purpose.) I limited myself to appearances with hosts who lack social capital or clout or whatever it's called these days. It was the only way I could imagine a pleasant conversation.

What would become of this reclusion if I became a professor again? Would I have to start doing the personal brand bullshit? I didn't think so—my infamy was already a brand in itself, albeit an unfavorable one—but I had to consider this type of stuff before making any move. I was clear about one thing: I wouldn't bother applying for the job unless I knew that I would accept it. I was out of patience with uncertainty.

After Diana returned from work, I told her about the job ad, rambling more than a Led Zeppelin song. She waited patiently for me to verbalize my neuroses.

"So, yeah, anyway," I finished, "that's the situation. Should I do it?"

She raised her eyebrows and waved me away from the kitchen table.

"Fuck. Yes. Apply tonight."

■ ■ ■

I'm not kidding whenever I reference my neuroses. Applying to AUC evoked them in abundance. I immediately began running through dozens of scenarios, ranging from likely to practically impossible.

To begin with, I was friends with AUC's new president, Ahmad Dallal, whom I got to know well at AUB, where he served as provost before moving into a regular faculty position. (Ahmad, in fact, provided one of my "moral references" when I applied to be a bus driver, quite likely the only time a university president served as a referee in the history of Fairfax County's School Transportation Department.) Would I be ruining a friendship? Was it fair to potentially toss a hand grenade into the middle of his new tenure?

It's true. I actually considered the well-being of a university president. Nobody was more surprised about it than I. There was no choice, really. Through a mixture of fear, insecurity, and trauma, I always worry about the trouble I might cause other people. I hate that I'm a potential source of distress and misfortune because there are a million worse things a person can do than offer me a job, publish one of my articles, or invite me to give a speech. Doing any of those things is liable to get a person listed on the Zionist defamation site Canary Mission, or to cause that person tension with management. I've hated the tendency ever since the Illinois fiasco. It's bad enough to target political antagonists for recrimination; it seems like overkill to target bystanders, as well.

And what of my potential colleagues? The department to which I considered applying, English and Comparative Literature, only had five faculty members at the time, but I knew two of them. Was I putting them in a shitty position by sending in a dossier? What if they're left to handle a public controversy or pressure from powerful outside forces?

I knew all this was improbable and contained a whiff of self-importance. It's normal to imagine ourselves more consequential than we actually are, but I wasn't operating from some fantasy world. All the stuff that I worried about had already happened, more than once in some cases. I had to acknowledge the toxic possibilities embedded in my name. Over the years I've grown adept at recognizing the potential for unexpected problems.

That there were so many angles to contemplate for a simple job application illustrated anew that higher education can be a hellish environment. Notorious or not, nobody applies for an academic position without thinking about the politics of fit and representation.

I was somewhat familiar with AUC, which should have helped, but the familiarity only exacerbated my nerves. When I was at AUB (a separate institution despite the similar name), I traveled twice to Cairo. The first time was as a visiting writer in which I gave a few talks and met with students. The second, a year later, was to participate in an American Studies conference organized by the poet and translator Khaled Mattawa. I went as part of a group of AUB faculty and students. Both experiences were good. I loved Cairo. The AUB contingent stayed in the old Ramses Hilton, which was the epitome of 1970s luxury. It felt like we had walked into a Sadat-era telenovela. It was pretty much perfect.

I wanted to go back.

With Diana's encouragement, I sent the application.

Less than six weeks later, after a lot of time on Zoom, I was offered the job.

■ ■ ■

I'm not unusually prone to worry. I know it seems that I am because worrying is a motif I keep returning to, but by and large I probably don't worry nearly as much as I should. Just as I hit send on the email accepting my new job as professor of English and Comparative Literature at the American University in Cairo, the second-guessing began.

What the fuck did you just do?

Did you really think this thing through?

My immediate worry was that a few months later I'd be sitting in new faculty orientation, tyrannized by PowerPoint, and suddenly realize that I'd made an enormous mistake. Already I was trying to rewire my brain to a prior incarnation that I swore I'd never deal with again. There was no switch to flip. I'd have to reacclimate the hard way.

I was tremendously productive while bus driving but cultivated no measurable productivity—the kind of stuff that institutions like to accumulate for metrics and reputation. It was an uncommon situation. There were no departmental standards to satisfy, no grants and awards to chase, no imaginary (and ever-changing) barometers for the job market. I produced material if I wanted to and if I didn't, then I only had to answer to my own disappointment. I wasn't enamored of this individualistic sensibility, but any residual faith in the notion of an intellectual community on campus had long ago expired. My people were now disaffected academics and low-volume Twitter accounts contemptuous of social climbing.

That freedom was about to end. I would again have to fill in annual reports listing all my accomplishments. Assessment was fixing to rejoin my vocabulary. I'd have to feign interest in theoretical babble. My CV would need regular updating. I didn't even want to contemplate receptions and dinner parties.

But why? What in the world would compel me to discard a hard-earned freedom?

I could name lots of reasons, some more convincing than others, but the answer exists in the question: getting the hell out of the United States was by far the greatest attraction.

The transition from academic to school bus driver was mostly smooth; despite the counterintuitive trajectory, something about it made sense. The inverse—going from school bus driving to academe—is a lot bumpier. This is especially so if the driver knows what to expect.

With a contract in hand, I was struck by a need to publish again. It wasn't altogether a bad thing. Suddenly, I was motivated to write a few more (nonfiction) books and had a ton of material ready to go. I remembered that being a professor wasn't all headaches and indignity. I had actually enjoyed a few things about it. A distinct reality kept invading my senses, in all its illogic and unlikelihood: I was no longer anxious. My restlessness had found a home.

About that contract: it never felt secure to me, despite having read it closely for potential loopholes and finding it ironclad. (Is there even such a thing as an ironclad contract?). I accepted the job in late December 2021, and deferred the start date from spring semester, 2022, until fall. That left a lot of time for mendacity. When the details had been sorted, and the hire was on the books, I asked the folks at AUC to keep it quiet. They agreed that being mum was a good idea.

There was a great magnitude to the secrecy. I told only family and close friends, comforted by the fact that none of my relations used Twitter. I had no clue whether Zionists and politicians would raise a fuss, but I wasn't willing to take a chance. I would return to academe in the same condition of fugitivity from whence I was expelled. Fear of reprisal wasn't the only motivating factor; I wasn't ready to answer questions about the decision—I had no answers to provide. And I wanted to make sure that the announcement, should it be forced into existence, had utility beyond my own little situation.

From the moment that the Illinois fiasco became a public event, I tried to avoid tabloid rituals and to de-emphasize individuality. My firing arose from Palestine and originated in North America. Repression of unpopular ideas is a normal practice of colonization, and only in meticulous, unapologetic analysis can individuals harmed by that practice potentially find relief. With the rise of social media, every twerp and dweeb with a smartphone discovered that clambering about being repressed is a great way to generate a following. (Big Tech! Deep State! Russians!) I was adamant that mine wasn't ultimately a problem of repression. Nor was the problem mine alone. It was a byproduct of imperial rot that demanded a radical response.

Getting fired can be an excellent career move if you aren't really bothered by scruples. Just lurch to the right and bellow about left-wing cancel culture and it won't be long until you score an invite to the Joe Rogan Experience, get written up by three different *New York Times* columnists, enjoy the hero treatment from free-speech Twitter, and have your very own Substack that sounds exactly like all the other ones. This extremely common trajectory is no doubt annoying, but it becomes downright sinister in light of its consequences. By transforming themselves into individual martyrs, putative victims of repression sell themselves to the same illiberal forces that they claim to deplore. They are taken up as heroes by centers of power and in turn serve power with tremendous efficacy. The disenfranchised people from whom the martyr extracts credibility are systematically excluded from the conversation.

If you ever find yourself a victim of recrimination—legitimate recrimination, deriving from the ruling class—then the mandate should be to embrace your wretchedness. At least then you won't have given yourself to the oppressor.

The ruling class never merely punishes individuals. It punishes vulnerable targets from within persecuted communities. Ongoing colonization of Native nations in North and South America informed my troubles because the field in which I had been hired, Indigenous Studies, offered no value to the corporate university. Zionist colonization of Palestine was likewise integral to the troubles because it entails retribution against Israel's critics. I've scarcely made a decision for eight years without these factors in mind. It was in service to the dispossessed that I refused to moderate my politics or apologize for them.

I wanted my return to academe to be an occasion for defiance, not conciliation. It would be bad for multiple parties if the usual reactionary forces interfered.

Suddenly, I had to manage my public persona with more caution. At least that's what close friends told me. "For God's sake, man, stay the fuck away from Twitter until you're already in Cairo." They didn't always put it so bluntly, but that was the gist of their advice.

It wasn't bad advice. Hell, it was without question the sensible thing to do, the responsible course of action. I had no doubt about it and still didn't listen. Well, maybe I'm overstating my stupidity. I did heed the warnings, but I didn't quit tweeting altogether. I also continued publishing essays on my website, irregularly as always.

I wasn't defying my friends' counsel. To the contrary, I remained acutely cognizant of my precarious situation. I just didn't want to completely muzzle myself for something as trivial as an academic job. I'm aware that the compulsion to yammer in ways that invite trouble is a personality flaw, but I like to tell myself there's a principle involved.

It wasn't the same anymore, though. Gone was the silent cackle in my brain as political antagonists had yet another conniption: "Go ahead, motherfucker. Call my boss." Gone as well was the sense that negative judgment had no material effect on the life of my family. Now my comments were subject to the tacit approval of colleagues and administrators.

We're never truly free to speak. That's one of the many myths arising from a religious devotion to "free speech" in the United States. Speech has social effects and consequences and those are enough to limit the range of content, depending on the situation. Never mind corporate or political restrictions. When situations change, so do the limits. Maintaining an academic career as an opponent of Zionism means being sharply mindful of vigorous limitations. Such limitations are less severe for a school bus driver or an independent writer (i.e., being unemployed). Certain forms of speech will always evoke negative consequences no matter their legal status, particularly those supportive of Indigenous liberation or revolutionary violence.

People know exactly what the limits are, too, in multiple situations. You can observe them adhering to those limitations all the time. I see well-known Palestinian scholar-activists (this is a negative descriptor, by the way) waving off claims that Israel engages in genocide; I see them hot and bothered about the Israeli occupation in supposed moments of calm, but quick to condemn armed Palestinian resistance; I see them offer nuanced talking points about foreign adversaries that just so happen to mimic the line coming out of Foggy Bottom. They deftly know how to tailor a critique to appeal to dueling audiences: those on the side of the dispossessed and the power brokers who maintain so much dispossession. Speakers with designs on upward mobility always moderate diction according to their economic station.

Really, you can discern the measure of political seriousness by online behavior. Whom does a person follow? Whom does a person retweet? Whom does a person respond to or ignore? All the clues are there. Social climbing on the left follows a distinct pattern: engage with enough subversives to cultivate a radical image and, after catching the attention of a superior demographic, leave the rabble behind. Palestine has long been used for this purpose. No proper anti-Zionist earns the adulation of elite universities or corporate media.

The anonymous and minor accounts that I follow and interact with suffer no such burden—or, better said, the restrictions they suffer are less burdensome than those of the aspiring pundit. I wanted to speak in a voice that's illegible (or objectionable) to audiences enthralled by US exceptionalism. Doing so as a professor is a difficult task.

I had to come to terms with the fact that I was traumatized from an eventful history on Twitter. I used to balk at the notion of trauma as a result of online shenanigans but have come to believe there's something to the idea. In fact, I would venture to guess that a lot of seemingly adjusted people are traumatized by online interaction. It's a bizarre world, noxious and irresistible. For me, the trauma (or whatever you want to call it) arises from having my tweets scrutinized by journalists, intellectuals, and legal bodies. I can't send one without thinking about it being forever plastered to my body like a bulbous mole.

The attention itself probably traumatized me. I reckon I wasn't exactly built for it. But when your ability to earn a living is contingent upon the approval of strangers prone to hostility, attention can be more than an unwelcome or exhilarating incident. It becomes a continuous threat and a component of everyday identity. I hated that I couldn't make a public comment without a fearful aftermath. Try as I might, I couldn't shake the usual questions. What would this tweet look like in a court of law? How will this tweet perform if five thousand professors give it a close reading? Will it be easy for dishonest readers to twist this tweet into something malevolent?

Tweeting at all felt horribly irresponsible. What if I got fired from yet another job because of anti-Zionism on the platform? Who would possibly defend me this time around? "You dumbshit," they'd say. "Why were you on Twitter?" Because Twitter leads only to bad things. Because it's proper to trade silence for job security. Because Twitter means you're asking for it.

Because the people doing the repressing apparently should be absolved.

I was caught between these two inimical ways of thinking: of course I shouldn't be using Twitter or saying anything, period; I should stay completely out of sight. At the same time, there's no way a potential academic employer could be ignorant of my online persona. It's not that I believe using social media is some grand gesture of rebellion. Those media are mostly silly and toxic, as is the incessant slogan "I will not be silenced!" It's more what the silence would represent. I occasionally like to comment on something meaningful to me and don't think that suppressing ideological compunctions to accommodate the inherent conservativism of academic institutions is especially virtuous or healthy.

I'm well aware of the boundaries governing suitable professorial commentary and keep crossing them, anyway. I'm not trying to court attention or martyr myself. Nor am I optimistic about the usefulness of punditry. Most of the time I remain speechless, cooped up in my own secretive habitat, which does nothing to mitigate the disquiet. I don't hang my identity on speechlessness or provocation. I'm simply trying to find purpose in a world unwelcoming of both sonance and silence.

AUC hired me because I was eminently qualified for the position it advertised and because I handled myself well during the interview process. But hiring a professor is always about esoteric subtexts and unstated qualifications. For better or worse, I needed to know that AUC was also prepared to appoint my big mouth to an academic position.

■ ■ ■

An assertive person drives the bus. Passengers on the bus are passive or apathetic. When you screw somebody over, you've thrown them under the bus. Sometimes you take a moment to put the bus in reverse, just to drive the point home. In order not to miss out on something awesome, you need to get on the bus. If you don't get on the bus, you're dodging responsibility.

Don't be dishonest. It's not cool to take people for a ride. Come on! Be decisive! You don't want to just be riding along.

Be warned. A scumbag is liable to run you over with the bus. Bad decisions mean you've boarded the wrong bus.

Remember, though: the bus doesn't drive itself. Dilly-dally too much and the bus will leave the station.

And yet I can't think of a metaphor that describes the current state of my life. I'm off the goddamn bus altogether.

■ ■ ■

I remember when I defended my dissertation. For six years I tried to imagine the relief and euphoria of that moment. The moment arrived and failed to initiate the galactic changes that were lodged in my imagination. I was still Steve, still the exact same shy and skeptical person. The only difference was that I could add a title to my name when booking hotel rooms and airline tickets.

Alan Velie and Robert Warrior were at my defense, of course, along with Catherine John, James Treat, and the late Daniel Cottom, one of the smartest human beings I've ever known (and a terrific teacher). A small crowd turned up to watch the proceedings in Gittinger Hall's conference room. I worried that Robert would ask difficult questions and maybe express displeasure with my answers (which I assumed would suck), but, always the champion of my work, he was more interested in discussing the implications of my thesis than exposing my theoretical shortcomings. Alan was, well, Alan: outwardly grumpy but filled with a generosity of spirit that all grad students should be able to experience (but in too many cases don't).

I gave my spiel, answered the questions, and was subsequently welcomed into the club to halting applause from the audience. Instead of uncontainable joy, I felt like going back to my apartment to do a crossword puzzle. The moment wasn't anticlimactic so much as strikingly anodyne. I had reverted to my authentic self.

I was happy, don't get me wrong. And definitely relieved. The actual feeling wasn't up to the anticipation, that's all. Big moments rarely function like that. The excitement exists in the lead-up, or in an unexpected aftermath.

There was plenty to be excited about for the near future. I would be getting married that June and starting on tenure track at the University of Wisconsin–Whitewater a few months later. The upper Midwest was alien to me, but UWW was enough like Radford that I didn't anticipate any great surprises.

The anticipation was half correct. The marriage went well, but my professional life would never fail to surprise me.

. . .

It was the third time I had braved the line at the Franconia DMV. The first was to take my test for a CDL learner's permit. The second was to retake the test because I didn't study the first time. As on the two prior occasions, it was cold and damp as I waited in a line wrapping around two sides of the building. (For the second visit, I thought I could beat the crowd by rising early and arriving a few minutes before the DMV opened—the idea wasn't as novel as I had imagined.)

This time, high spirits helped alleviate the wait. I was there to collect my regular CDL license. I'd heard others in my cohort complaining about snags and delays, which nagged at me as I finally made it inside the building and waited on a plastic chair. I hated the idea of doing the same thing over again. I was so close to finishing and giddy at the possibility of actually putting the license in my wallet.

The process was grueling at times, and I watched numerous people fall short of the goal. Training for the CDL was the first time that I behaved as a serious student. I was diligent in grad school, but that entailed a different type of studying: reading novels and critical texts and writing lots of papers. I'm talking about old-fashioned studying: memorizing information and then having to apply it on an exam. I'd never done it. Take what you will from the fact that I ended up with a doctorate.

The automated voice finally called my number and I jog-walked to the counter and explained why I was there.

"They told me that they'd send the information to you."

"Mmm."

"I mean, like, I passed the road test and stuff, with the county. They were supposed to tell you."

"Mmm."

"I had to back the bus up between cones and everything."

The woman on the other side of the counter looked at me for the first time. "Nice."

"They also told me to tell you that the license should say no restrictions. I'm not even sure what that means, but, yeah, no restrictions."

"I know."

"Cool. Thank you."

"You gonna keep that thing on?"

It took me a second to realize that she meant my winter coat.

"I guess so. There really isn't any place to put it."

"For your picture."

"What picture?" Then it occurred to me what she was saying. "I'm getting the license?"

The woman closed her eyes a bit too long for a blink. "Stand over here, next to the gray screen."

"I thought you'd use the same picture from my learner's."

"Don't smile, look straight ahead."

Five minutes later I walked out the door with a brand-new CDL in my coat pocket. I smiled at everyone in line as I headed to my car. Once inside, I let out an enormous whoop. I wasn't anticipating so much joy in that moment. It felt better than getting my first driver's license at sixteen.

CDL in hand, I went down to the area office and filled in the paperwork to complete my hire. That same afternoon I began my very own route. I'll always consider acquiring the CDL sixteen years after defending my dissertation an essential academic accomplishment.

■ ■ ■

He no longer calls me "papa." I'm "dad" now, a spartan, utilitarian term. It's okay. I sort of like being dad. It gives me license to make a certain kind of joke.

I see the pictures from only a few years ago and he looks small and innocent, pudgy and cherubic despite his height—a perfect little boy. Now he towers over his soccer teammates, running with a loping, awkward gait. The fashionable haircut for boys is long on top and cropped around the sides and back, just as it was when I was a teenager. He wears a mess of curls tumbling down his forehead and mostly obscuring the neatly sheared hair beneath them. In a certain posture or particular light he looks like a young adult, or like a college freshman when he sprawls on the couch without a shirt and watches television. He still has little boy moments, and they're lovely, but those moments are slowly being overwhelmed by a brain increasingly attuned to independence. He's no longer my little man, my shadow, my BFF—not always, anyway. He'll still take my hand sometimes when we're walking to the store, still curl next to me on the couch, still ask wonderfully incoherent questions that could have come from the mouth of a toddler. He's becoming a man and nothing I can perceive in this life makes me prouder. It's grand enough to supersede the impending loneliness.

After the pandemic hit and I quit driving, he began asking what I do. He knows very well what I do in the day-to-day because he usually participates, so I understood him to mean, "What do you do for a living?" He had already learned to ask the country's most important question in all its undertones and implications. "Your papa is a writer," Diana would interject before I had a chance to answer. I was relieved when she did, because I didn't know what kind of answer would satisfy the curiosity of a child seeking something direct and comprehensible. Children have a specific idea of what grown-ups "do." We're firefighters or doctors or schoolteachers or cops. "Unpublished author" or "former-professor-turned-former-bus-driv-er-turned-househusband" is a bit beyond their comprehension. It's beyond the comprehension of most adults, as well.

Grown-ups age along with children, not always so visibly, but in a steady diminution, nonetheless. It seems like an entirely different chronology, but each party's sense of time relies on the other's meta-morphosis: youth and senescence; energy and fatigue; innocence and weariness. I know I'll die soon. I can feel it in my body. My chest aches at the heart and arteries. The pain spreads all the way to my fingers and toes, producing a feeling of negation that overwhelms any semblance of vigor. I want to make it long enough to get back into the classroom and complete the work filling my hard drive. After that, I can sense an impulse to die. If I'm wrong, then I'll need to learn how to relax.

But the child. I can't imagine that I'll ever tire of watching him exist, magnificent in all epochs, a vessel of joy in each stage of mat-uration. I don't want to deprive him of my presence. I don't want to leave him alone in a world so apt to cruelty and privation. But I don't know how to keep my body solvent. It's a terrible predicament, more onerous than any having to do with career or identity.

Parenthood changed my own memories of childhood, too. Once I had a son, I could better see things my parents' way. I could finally understand the agony of loving imperfect creatures. I have a sense now of what it must be like having a child who didn't want to go out and play, who seemed to invite the world's darkness, who made bad grades on principle, who insisted on self-destruction as a form of rebellion. I could recognize the distress of having a child too timid and traumatized to communicate. Because I don't tell them anything. I don't tell anyone anything (except you, dear reader; you, I tell everything). They learn about my life through my website and social media. Before the website and social media, it was a lot of guesswork, I suppose. Avoiding others isn't a solitary choice; it's always a communal affair.

Despite the flaws and foibles I recognized as I grew older, the tensions that arose from my deviant second-generation trajectory, I'm proud of my parents. In moments of intense loneliness or extended detachment, my heart delivering worrisome shoots of pain into my gut and shoulder, I sometimes yearn to be little again so I can amble forward and cry into their laps. That's all a child can really ask of their parents, the momentary promise of security in a scary, unsafe civilization. And I realize in these shimmers of yearning that that's what I want more than anything from this life, for my child to one day be proud of me.

The constitutional motif of the United States isn't freedom or equality. It is redemption. From the Puritan settlers to the Civil Rights Movement to the paragons on Capitol Hill, the country is presented as a beatific, immortal organism of godly provenance, lush and abundant, a repository of hope for the poor and battered. It is the apotheosis of grace. It is sunshine inside a cavern. It is a grove of date palms in the desert. It is, above all, an idea to be redeemed. Everywhere its champions and critics profess fidelity to some form of redemption. Those who suffer, blessed by celestial tenacity, will rise in victory. It is a compelling story entirely reliant on belief over evidence. Under the reign of capitalism, we don't get the resurrection, only the suffering.

School

Like all August days in northeast Africa, the morning arrives bright and sweltering. I slip into the bathroom for a cold shower and, after finishing, immediately get on my laptop. I want to make sure, for the hundredth time, that everything is in order. Bus schedule. Roster. Building. Room number. I wasn't so fitful last time around, but I haven't done this for a while and have been experiencing vivid nightmares about missing the entire semester.

I hear my son up and about. He soon barges into the living room in a pair of baggy athletic shorts and a Ronaldo jersey. I think he looks unkempt, but he insists that it's the normal style these days. He's been in school for a couple of weeks already. From what I've seen of his classmates, a gaggle of little Messis and Salahs, he isn't lying.

Diana stepped into the shower shortly after I exited, as per her custom in the month since we arrived. I move to the dining room table with my son as he eats a bowl of Cinnamon Toast Crunch. I urge him to try zaatar instead, but he waves off the suggestion. "That stuff costs an arm and a leg in this country," I tell him, nodding toward his bowl. He shrugs and keeps spooning soppy cereal into his mouth. He understands, and even empathizes, but knows I'm just trying to guilt him into better health.

Diana has emerged by the time he finishes and we gather his things for school. He just began fifth grade and doesn't need us to accompany him—the school is across the road—but we like walking along and our presence doesn't seem to bother him. We descend four flights of stairs, breathing in dry, dusty heat, and make our way across the relatively quiet street to the school's gated entryway. We beep open the iron door with IDs attached to lanyards and walk to the edge of the elementary building. We each give him a quick hug, just enough to express affection without embarrassment, and head back to the apartment.

We live in Maadi, a verdant residential area in the south of Cairo, billed as a respite from the crowded chaos uptown. Maadi is pleasant, but plenty chaotic. It has trees and some parkland—adorned with date palms, jacaranda, cypress, and eucalyptus—but it's still an urban neighborhood with high density and bustling street life. It's not far enough from the city center to spare its residents noise and pollution. The pollution I could do without; the noise is an unexpected blessing. Less than a week after arriving, I remembered how infrequently I felt lonely in Beirut because the sounds of the city surrounded me. I like hearing the noises of a society when they're not in focus.

So far, we've enjoyed it. The Nile corniche isn't far, although a sizable walk, and there's a huge maze of streets to explore. As in Beirut, we enjoy comfortable circumstances amid widespread poverty. There's nothing to do about it but feel guilty and stay out of the way when the next revolution arrives.

Back at the apartment, we settle across from one another at the dining room table.

"Are you ready?" Diana asks.

"Not really."

She's offered multiple times to come along, but I reckon it'll only make me antsier. I shouldn't be nervous—I never used to be, not even at twenty-one—but I can't control the sensation and don't feel like trying to sort its provenance. I'll just stay nervous.

I do know that I'm not simply trying something different, something familiar but entirely new. Today is also the realization of a principle. Perhaps it's a foolish devotion, a delusional and passive vengeance, but I'm committed to it with my entire chest. I never liked the idea of keeping out of places the oppressor has declared off-limits.

I stand and begin collecting my stuff. I'll arrive at the bus stop early, an upshot of my nervousness. Diana gives me a long hug and whispers much-needed words of encouragement. She decides to walk me down. I don't object. We head three blocks to Victoria Square amid a canopy of balconies and palm fronds and wait for the bus that will take me from Maadi to New Cairo. We're the first people there.

Others soon arrive. They cannot tolerate silence because they're professors and begin chitchatting in that self-important cadence that I've hated for twenty years. Well, I remind myself, you gave up the right to sneer; they are once again your people. I smile and toss in a few words. I haven't arrived at campus, but I'm already on the job.

The square (actually an oval) is busy with motorbikes and micro-buses and taxis honking in rapid bursts. Pedestrians weave through the traffic with an intuition that takes years to master. Soon the bus appears and creeps around the fat part of the turnabout. Diana squeezes my hand and assures me that everything will be fine. Air brakes hiss as the bus lurches to a stop. I fall into line and shuffle along. Halfway up the steps, I turn and wave at Diana. She wears a proud and pensive expression that I have seen many times before.

I manage to get myself into an empty row and immediately open a novel. (I'll never tire of reading on buses.) This bus promises Wi-Fi, but I've never been on a moving vehicle with consistent internet. I don't pay much attention to the book. I keep staring out the window, assessing my new surroundings. Egypt is a complex place. I have no desire to front as an expert. I'm a guest in the country and intend to behave accordingly. It's beautiful to my eyes, that's for sure. I adore the khaki and ecru tones of the arid landscape. My main goal is to stay alive. Cultivating a sense of peace in this vivid, achromatic world is my short-term strategy. So far, I've been able to overlook the heavy development cluttering the scenery between Old and New Cairo.

Forty-five minutes into my journey, the bus pulls up to one of AUC's many gates. I show my ID to the security guard and pass through the turnstile. The campus is lovely, filled with water features, ornate tiling, and prismatic flowers. It still has a new vibe, a sense of anodyne novelty, but over fifteen years it's developed enough shabbiness to make it feel more inviting. I'm wearing an old OU ball cap and can still feel the sun landing on my scalp.

I keep my head down as I walk, accustomed to being noticed in my two previous jobs. Quick glances to the left and right show that

I'm being paranoid or narcissistic. Nobody knows who I am. The situation is similar to my first day at UW-Whitewater. I'm just a guy on his way to some banal assignment like everyone else on campus. There's nothing to worry about. I worry, anyway.

Smoking isn't allowed on campus—in Egypt!—and so I look around for an isolated nook where I can introduce more nicotine into my nervous system. I find a quiet, shady spot behind the student center and imbibe without peeking at a book or computer. Hot air makes smoking uncomfortable, but I do manage to feel more relaxed by the time I finish. I toss the extinguished butt into a trash bin and walk to my building. I have a little while to mess around on the internet before class begins. Once in my office—sparsely decorated and likely to stay that way—I recheck my rosters and room assignments. Nothing's changed in the last two hours.

Twitter elevates my worry to pre-nicotine levels and so I browse true crime on Reddit. Not much of interest. No vital mysteries have been solved today.

It's almost time. Excitement starts to balance my terror. For reasons I don't understand, I'm not feeling the usual symptoms of anxiety. I have an appetite and no pain anywhere in my abdomen. My mind isn't foggy. Every other aspect of my physiology tingles with feeling.

Is it the struggle going away? Is that why I worry? The circle's closed. It's the final station. I've reached the end of the line. Insert your own geometrical cliché. I got what I really, truly wanted; something I wanted so much I couldn't admit to wanting it. It's both anticlimactic and ominous.

The work itself doesn't make me uneasy. I scarcely view it as work, to be honest. When AUC assigned me three classes for my first semester, I laughed at how easy it seemed. (Professors consider three courses a semester an above-average workload; adjuncts often teach five.) I don't have tenure and so there's no good reason to view my new situation as permanent.

I guess I don't want to confront the fact that I continue to feel shame for never having resolved my ambiguity. My mind insists on welcoming this damnable condition. Ambiguity is where sensation resides and I long ago realized that the one constraint I cannot survive is dullness.

This is what you always wanted, I keep insisting. Ever since you were a little boy at your father's hip. You loved the chemical smell of dad's lab on campus, the cinder block walls of the classroom building, the chalkboard dust covering your fingers. You would hang out in his office, in awe of the entire scene: a desk crowded with papers, a bookshelf cluttered with science trinkets, and dad gruff and serious in his green swivel chair. You would grab his hand as he led you to an empty classroom to pass the time playing teacher. He always kissed you on the top of the head, told you to behave. There were no antagonists in this extraordinary space. It was a world apart from civilization.

For all those years you thought that you were heeding his command, that you were behaving, but your conduct was merely a prelude to disgrace, a sentiment he would never admit out loud even though you could always feel it. He was so proud when you told him about AUC, said that he was relieved, that it didn't matter if you were leaving the country. He'd miss you, but it was okay. He considered it worthwhile. He hasn't been to Egypt since the early 1960s, on his way to America. He's excited to see it again. He remembers the trains; people were hanging onto the sides of the boxcars. He'll come visit. Goddammit this is good news. He can now die happy. You are sad because this elation has revealed the depth of his sorrow. You understand the subtext underlying his sudden logorrhea, that for nearly a decade he has endured shame and odium, but his happiness isn't guaranteed because you still might die first. That familiar pain has returned to your chest. Your breathing is restricted. Airflow stops at the bottom of your neck and you struggle to supply enough oxygen to your diaphragm. You sense movement in this state of dislocation. It is suddenly very hot, with bright light everywhere. You hear a murmur of voices close and distant. You have a vague sense of cement and orange trees, of snack shacks, of chlorinated water. A blast of chilly air abruptly buffets your face. Then sounds of laughter. Doors slamming. Footfall on ceramic tile. And just like that you're in front of a classroom filled with youngsters. They look up at you with expressions somewhere between expectation and indifference. They are young and dressed in various degrees of formality. They come into focus as actual beings, flesh and blood, lined up in orderly little rows. This is it, you tell yourself. This is where it ends.

You stand and smile. The confusion vanishes.

"Good morning," you say, steady and cheerful. "My name is Steve. And from here on out I'll be your professor."

Steven Salaita is Professor of English and Comparative Literature at the American University in Cairo. He writes at stevesalaita.com.